More
Royal
Ruby

Philip Hopper

Photography by Bruce Waters

4880 Lower Valley Road, Atglen, PA 19310 USA

Dedication

I am dedicating this book to all the glassware collectors throughout the world. My greatest reward for writing the book has been the friendships I have developed while displaying glassware or autographing books at shows, talking to people on the internet, or meeting people at antique shops, flea markets, or auctions. I can share their excitement when they tell me about finding a rare piece of glass or one with a label. Writing the book has been one of the most rewarding experiences in my life!

Book Design by Anne Davidsen
Type set in Zapf Chancery/ Souvenir Light

ISBN: 0-7643-0870-X
Printed in China
1 2 3 4

Published by Schiffer Publishing Ltd.
4880 Lower Valley Road
Atglen, PA 19310
Phone: (610) 593-1777; Fax: (610) 593-2002
E-mail: Schifferbk@aol.com
Please visit our web site catalog at **www.schifferbooks.com**

This book may be purchased from the publisher.
Include $3.95 for shipping.
Please try your bookstore first.
We are interested in hearing from authors
with book ideas on related subjects.
You may write for a free catalog.

In Europe, Schiffer books are distributed by
Bushwood Books
6 Marksbury Rd.
Kew Gardens
Surrey TW9 4JF England
Phone: 44 (0)181 392-8585; Fax: 44 (0)181 392-9876
E-mail: Bushwd@aol.com

Contents

Acknowledgments

This book would never have been published without the help of numerous glassware collectors and friends nationwide. I would like to make special tribute to several collectors. Rick Hirte (Sparkle Plenty Glassware, Bar Harbor Maine) loaned me two Banded Ring tumblers, located several rare pieces of Royal Ruby for the book, promoted my first book on Royal Ruby on his website, and thought of adding a ruler to the book for the convenience of the collector. Dr. Leonette Walls (Gardendale, Alabama) loaned me the Royal Ruby ashtray painted by Dean Mogle. Finally, Kate Puhl was kind enough to sell me the four Inspiration Royal Ruby ice tea glasses which belonged to her grandmother.

A very special "thanks" to Barbara W. Birge (Lexington, Kentucky) who not only located glassware for the book, but accompanied me on many glass buying trips throughout the Ohio Valley. Barb put up with my obsession and constant "babbling" about glassware. She was very gracious when I visited Lexington and totally filled her kitchen, dining room, one bedroom, and computer room with glassware, bottles, boxes, and packing materials. Like a flower in a field of weeds, Barb has been the "flower" in my life. She has been a great friend, always supported me in all my endeavors, and been there when I needed a shoulder to cry on. I feel blessed and thank God each day for allowing me to experience the total love and devotion of another person even so late in my life. I would hope that when she reads this, she will consent to share all that life has to offer and be my "partner for life."

I would also like to thank many of the present and former employees of Anchor Hocking for helping me identify and document information about Royal Ruby glassware. I want to express my sincere appreciation to David A. Bates for providing insight on glass batch formulation and the "striking" process and Paul Stuart for identifying many of the unlisted pieces of Royal Ruby glassware.

Once again, I would like to thank the people at Schiffer Publishing Ltd. for making this project another very enjoyable and memorable experience.

Introduction

Collecting is by definition the constant accumulation or gathering of a particular item or items over an extended period of time. My collecting Royal Ruby glassware has surpassed the "collecting stage" and really has become an obsession. Once I completed my book *Royal Ruby*, I was obsessed with expanding my collection of glassware and Anchor Hocking documentation. I found so many new pieces of glassware that I thought it was only fitting to share my "finds" with everyone. Peter Schiffer and I decided to publish a second book on Anchor Hocking's Royal Ruby glassware, rather than wait a couple of years until *Royal Ruby* is updated. Hence you now have *More Royal Ruby*.

This new book contains some truly rare and interesting pieces of glassware. However, I am sure more will surface as time goes on. I have already located over 40 pieces of Royal Ruby glassware that are not in either book. I sincerely hope you will enjoy seeing the glassware as much as I did finding it.

Colored Glassware

I have included pieces of glassware in colors other than Royal Ruby to clarify production dates, show other sizes of items that may exist is Royal Ruby, or to document glass production. For example, I included the crystal High Point and 1952 catalog page to show the pattern was not produced just in the 1940s, as generally thought. If the crystal was produced in the 1950s, the Royal Ruby may have also been produced at this time.

Emblem Size

When Anchor Hocking changed the "batch" formula for Royal Ruby glass from gold to a mixture of copper, tin, and bismuth, they also changed the size of the familiar "anchor over H" mark that was embedded in the glass. The larger mark which is approximately one-quarter inch high indicates glass made with gold. When the "batch" formula was changed, the size of the emblem was reduced to approximately one-eighth inch. This is why you will see the larger emblem on the 6-inch straight shells made in the 1940s, and the smaller emblems on Provincial (Bubble) pieces made in the 1960s.

Ruby Flashing

A cheaper method of producing Royal Ruby items was to simply coat the piece of glass with a colored lacquer. Even though these are not "true" Royal Ruby, I have included ruby "flashed" items in the book because they are often the only way items received a red color. Several Wexford items appear red but were only flashed and "true" Royal Ruby items were never produced. Many of the lamps made with the 4-inch and 6-inch ivy balls were produced in both the Royal Ruby and flashed versions. The large apothecary jar has only been found in flashed colors (Forest Green and Royal Ruby) and one bottle, the mold #63-75 whiskey bottle, was flashed and only 34 made.

The flashing on glass will peel off quite readily. Sometimes it is very difficult to find pristine flashed items. When I bought a rare ruby flashed Soft Drink Convention commemorative bottle recently, the flashing was ruined when the overzealous cashier ripped off the price tag (attached to the bottle with tape). My pristine bottle now had a 1 1/2-inch square-shaped ragged clear spot, which diminished the bottle's value considerably!

Boxed Sets

I recently received a 22-piece set of R-4000 glassware where the contents of the box had been removed for packing prior to shipping. The seller indiscriminately removed the glassware and never paid any attention to the arrangement of the glassware in the box. It literally took me several hours to "solve the puzzle" and get everything correctly repacked. So others do not have the same problems I experienced, I have included overhead views of boxed sets so you can see how the glassware is arranged.

Light Analysis

There are few records that can be used to determine the manufacturer of a particular piece of glass. There is one fundamental fact about each company's glassware which can be used to determine the manufacturer. Each company producing red glass used a different metal or combination of metals to "strike" the red color. Although the red colors in the glass from different companies looks the same to the naked eye, each specific color is chemically different and each metal in the glass will absorb visible light at different frequencies. Using this basic principle, it is possible to definitively determine the chemical (metal) content of the glass and its manufacturer. Below is the actual test data from Anchor Hocking showing a comparison of the light transmission spectrums (curves) of Anchor Hocking's Royal Ruby glass and Wheaton Glass Company's red glass. You will notice the light transmission curves are totally different. If you were to run the same tests on Imperial, New Martinsville, Fenton, or other red glasses, you will see completely different curves. In the absence of definitive written proof, I am trying to access a light spectrophotometer to confirm certain pieces were, in fact, made by Anchor Hocking.

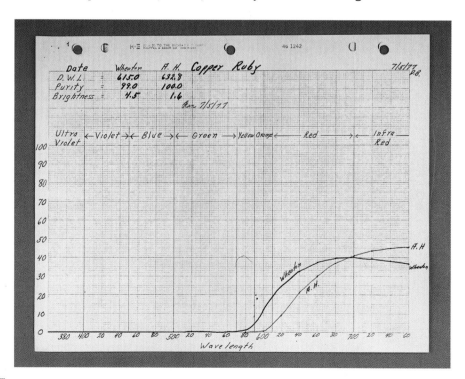

Spectrum data comparing the Wheaton and Anchor Hocking red glassware.

Baltic

The commonly found items are the "footed" glasses and bowls. The pattern has been listed in both the annual and institutional glassware catalogs, in crystal only, as recently as 1982.

Aftermarket relish set using three Baltic sherbets #R3313, $20-25.

Aftermarket relish server using four Baltic 12 oz. footed bowls #R3322, $40-50.

Baltic sherbet #R3313 and 6 1/4" sherbet plate #R828, $15-20 for both.

Left to right: Baltic cocktail shaker, 5 1/2" to top of chromed lid, $25-35; 3 1/2 oz. cocktail #R3312 marked with "me" as part of the shaker set, 2 5/8", $12-15. There was also another cocktail marked "you" as part of this set.

Baltic 6 1/4" sherbet plate #R828 with etched tulips, $12-15.

Banded Rings

Banded Rings was made in an assortment of colors and colored ring combinations. Banded Rings in Royal Ruby is very limited. I have only been able to locate three sizes of glasses and the 8" dinner plate in this color.

Banded Rings dinner plate, 8", $25-30.

Left to right: 10 oz. water tumbler, 5", $20-25; 8 oz. water tumbler, 4", $15-20; 5 1/2 oz. juice tumbler, 3", $15-20. *Ten-ounce water tumbler and juice tumbler courtesy of Rick Hirte.*

Beverly

This pattern was made in six sizes of glasses. The catalog lists the glasses in crystal. However, I have been able to find nine of the 4 1/2 oz. cocktails in Royal Ruby and one 9 oz. on-the-rocks in Forest Green. The *1967 Anchor Hocking Institutional Glassware* catalog does show the 12 oz. tumbler in Honey Gold.

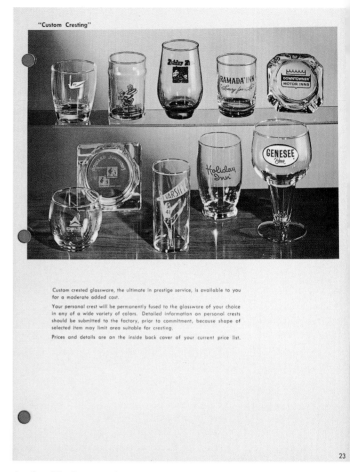

Anchor Hocking made Beverly in colors other than Royal Ruby. In addition to the Forest Green glass, the *1967 Anchor Hocking Institutional Glassware* catalog also pictured the Beverly glass in Honey Gold on the inside back cover.

Beverly 4 1/2 oz. cocktail in Royal Ruby #R3264, 2 3/4", $10-12.

Aftermarket handle applied to the Beverly 9 oz. on-the-rocks #E3265. This handle may have been made for other sizes of Beverly glassware.

Charm

Charm (square) dinnerware was produced in the 1950s and given the R-2200 designation by Anchor Hocking. There are several references to the 9 1/4" dinner plate, but I have been unable to confirm its existence. Also, I have never seen either the 6" soup bowl or the 8" x 11" platter in Royal Ruby. I seriously doubt any of these exist. However, there is always the possibility some "test" pieces were made.

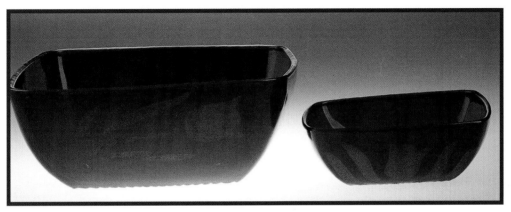

Charm bowls with etched tulips. Left to right: 7 1/2" salad bowl #R2277, $20-25; 4 3/4" dessert bowl #R2275, $12-15.

Aftermarket relish server using two 4 3/4" Charm dessert bowls #R2275, $15-20.

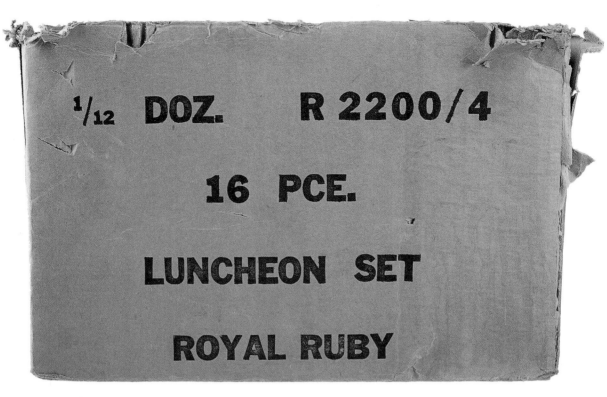

1/12 **DOZ.** **R 2200/4**

16 PCE.

LUNCHEON SET

ROYAL RUBY

16-piece Charm Luncheon Set #R2200/4 containing four cups #R2279, four saucers #R2229, four 4 3/4" dessert bowls #R2275, and four luncheon plates #R2241, $150-175.

Overhead view of the 16-piece set. You will notice the arrangement of the pieces in the box. The dessert bowls and saucers are placed vertically surrounding the cups. The luncheon plates are then placed on top to complete the set.

Chateau

This pattern was made in several colors and five sizes of glasses. I have been able to find the 12 oz. beverage glass in both Royal Ruby and Honey Gold. The Royal Ruby glass is not common and the dozen that I have been able to locate over the years are all marked with the "anchor over H" emblem embedded in the bottom of the glass.

Chateau 12 oz. beverage #R3332, 5 1/2", $12-15. This is an extremely heavy glass with the "anchor over H" embedded in the bottom of the glass.

New Color

CHATEAU

Handsome beverageware in a host of all-occasion sizes.

photo ref.	description	glass color	item order no.	BULK PACKED shipper doz. lbs.	
A	6½ oz. juice	Honey Gold	N3326	4	17
		Spicy Brown	Y3326	4	17
B	10 oz. on-the-rocks	Honey Gold	N3330	4	28
		Spicy Brown	Y3330	4	28
C	12 oz. beverage	Honey Gold	N3332	4	32
		Spicy Brown	Y3332	4	32
D	16½ oz. iced tea	Honey Gold	N3337	4	38
		Spicy Brown	Y3337	4	38
E	74 oz. pitcher	Honey Gold	N3364	½	21
		Spicy Brown	Y3364	½	21
		New Spearmint	G3364	½	21

36 Beverageware

Listing for Chateau glasses and pitcher listed in the *1978 Anchor Hocking Bulk Catalog.* Notice the glasses were made in four sizes and the pitcher is also used with the Newport tumblers listed later in this chapter. Only the 12 oz. beverage glass has been found in Royal Ruby.

Chateau 12 oz. beverage #N3332 in Honey Gold, 5 1/2", $12-15.

Early American Prescut

Even though Anchor Hocking made countless Early American Prescut pieces from 1960 to 1978, the company only made one piece in Royal Ruby, the 7 3/4" ash tray. The Royal Ruby ash tray is trademarked in the glass.

Photo of 55 mint condition EAPC ashtrays discovered in a secondhand glass shop in Lexington Kentucky.

I have always thought that we never know what treasures wait for us in the most unassuming places. This was the case on a recent trip to Lexington, Kentucky. I spent nine glorious days with my "significant other" checking out all the antique malls, antique shops, and flea markets in and around the Lexington area. On one rainy day we decided to drive and see what happens. We passed a salvage shop. You know the type. They buy "seconds," closeouts, and items most stores couldn't sell. This one looked like an old greenhouse converted into a store. Definitely not Wal-Mart or Saks Fifth Avenue! We went in, more out of curiosity than specifically looking for something. Down one aisle was glassware, another had baskets, and a third had plastic flowers and other knickknacks. Not the place you would expect to find anything "mind bending"! As luck would have it, I headed for the stacks of ashtrays under the glassware counter. I was awed by the number and variety of Anchor Hocking items here. As I pawed through the numerous piles of square ashtrays, I was completely oblivious to the two stacks of Anchor Hocking Early American Prescut Royal Ruby ashtrays in the back. Finally, as if struck by some "divine"

guidance, I turned my head and spied the EAPC ashtrays. I was speechless! For those of you who know me this was a feat in itself! As I stuttered and tried to convey my excitement to my "significant other," I noticed three additional piles of EAPC Royal Ruby ashtrays farther down the aisle. I was completely "tongue tied," my knees were shaking, and I couldn't believe the price of the ashtrays. I tried, with some success, to gain my composure and ask the lady at the checkout counter if they had the original boxes. To my disappointment, they said the ashtrays had been there for at least 15 years and they discarded the boxes long ago. The stock person, overhearing our conversation, said she thought there was still one box in the basement. I was able to convince her to check and lo and behold she returned with one dozen EAPC Royal Ruby ashtrays in the original box. I asked the price of the box of ashtrays, but she had to ask the manager. She returned and said I could have all I wanted for one half the marked price. I took all 55 ashtrays! They were absolutely mint and 51 were marked with the "anchor over H" emblem in the glass. I'm sure the entire staff was glad to see us and the ashtrays leave. They probably figured anyone who would buy 55 ashtrays must have a few "screws loose"! The Saturn car we were driving strained to hold the weight of all those ashtrays. We looked like modern day Beverly Hillbillies going to check out the "cement pond"! Even now, I get excited just thinking about that day. It just goes to show you that real finds are still out there!

No matter what anyone may tell you, even when you think you might have a complete collection, that's the time you will discover a previously unknown piece. This has certainly been my experience in over 27 years of collecting glassware, lithographs, marbles, handmade bottles, railroad tie date nails, etc. A certain well-known depression glass author quoted me as saying that I claimed to have everything ever made in Royal Ruby except one piece. The publication of *More Royal Ruby*, which consists of over 150 pieces collected since my first book, attests to the fact I would never make such a ludicrous statement. My professional training requires precise documentation of the facts and I would assume other authors hold the same high standards in their reference books.

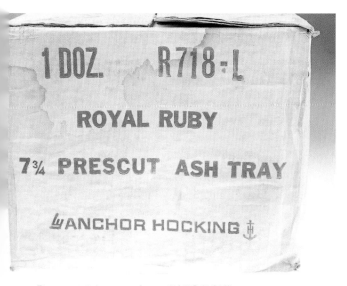

Box containing one dozen EAPC 7 3/4"
#R718-L ashtrays in Royal Ruby, $450-500.

Overhead view showing all 12 ashtrays in the box.

Fairfield

Anchor Hocking produced a variety of Fairfield colors through the years: avocado, honey gold, laser blue, sky blue, crystal, spearmint, smoke gray, spicy brown, and Royal Ruby. Royal Ruby pieces, given the R-1200 designation, appear to be one of the harder colors to find. Unlike all the other colors that were not trademarked, Royal Ruby pieces were trademarked.

The trademark, the familiar "anchor over H" emblem, is located on the side of the base of the relish dish and 5 1/4" two-handled bowl. On the compote, the trademark is located in the center of the base. There is a depression going up into the stem and the emblem is located in the depression.

Fairfield divided relish #R1250 mounted on a cast metal stand, $15-20.

Fortune

The Fortune pattern was produced from 1937 to 1938. While the majority of the pieces were produced in crystal and pink, the candy dish was made with a Royal Ruby cover. The Royal Ruby cover does not have the paneling normally found on the candy dish cover.

Fortune candy dish with the Royal Ruby lid in place. The Royal Ruby lids were placed on either a crystal or pink base, $15-20.

Fortune candy dish with the pink lid in place. Notice this lid is ribbed, unlike the plain Royal Ruby lid, $12-15.

Georgian

The Georgian pattern was probably produced from the 1940s to 1970s, but not continuously throughout this period. Unlike many of the other patterns of Royal Ruby, some of the tumblers have the "anchor over H" emblem embedded in the bottom of the glass. The tumblers tend to chip very easily, therefore, mint pieces will command a premium price. This is the only Royal Ruby pattern I know where Anchor Hocking made salt and pepper shakers.

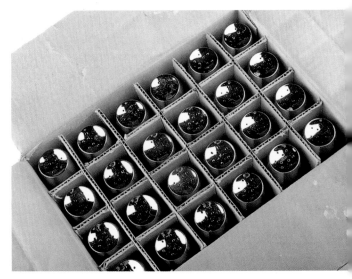

Overhead view showing 24 new Georgian salt and pepper shakers #R45.

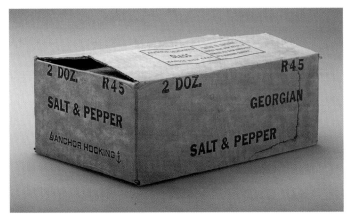

Full box containing 12 pairs of Georgian salt and pepper shakers #R45, $450-500; $50 for the box only.

High Point

High Point was another pattern made early in Anchor Hocking's history of Royal Ruby glass production. Produced in the 1940s and early 1950s, it had similar problems with very light red or clear areas in the glass. Most of the pieces in this pattern are uncommon. The 5 oz. and 9 oz. tumblers can be found, but the 13 oz. tumbler is rare. Until recently, I thought High Point was only made in Royal Ruby. I have found the 5 oz. fruit juice, 9 oz. table tumbler, and pitcher in crystal. The crystal High Point pattern is listed in the 1952 catalog.

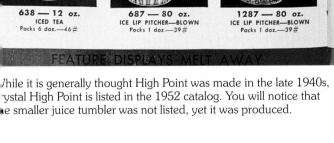

80 oz. High Point ice lip pitcher #1287 in crystal.

While it is generally thought High Point was made in the late 1940s, crystal High Point is listed in the 1952 catalog. You will notice that the smaller juice tumbler was not listed, yet it was produced.

High Point 9 oz. and 5 oz. tumblers in both Royal Ruby and crystal.

Left to right: water pitcher #R1287, 2 1/2 qt., $75-100; 13 oz. ice tea #R1208, 5 1/2", $35-40;
9 oz. table tumbler #R1201, 4 1/4", $12-15; 5 oz. fruit juice #R1203, 3 5/8", $10-15.

Hobnail

This was Anchor Hocking's first attempt to produce Royal Ruby glassware. Produced in the late 1930s, many of the pieces had very light red or clear areas. As I explained earlier in the book, the process of "striking" the ruby red color is extremely time, temperature, and batch formula dependent. It is evident the process had not been perfected when many of the Hobnail pitchers and tumblers were made.

Anchor Hocking made more than one size of Hobnail tumbler. Left to right: Hobnail pitcher #A2744, 60 oz., $30-35; 13 oz. tumbler, 5 1/2", $12-15; 9 1/2 oz. tumbler #A2719, 4 3/4", $8-10.

Factory bulletin introducing the Hobnail pitcher and glasses. The bulletin does not show the 13 oz. tumbler.

Inspiration

The Inspiration pattern was not part of Anchor Hocking's open stock. Most of the Inspiration glassware was given away as promotional items. Forest Green is the usual color found in this pattern. Inspiration was produced in five sizes. There was a limited "run" of the 13 oz. ice tea glass in Royal Ruby and very few were made. I have only seen five of the 13 oz. ice tea glasses in Royal Ruby and four of those are pictured below.

Inspiration 13 oz. ice tea in Royal Ruby, $80-100. Anchor Hocking made five sizes of Inspiration glasses. I have only been able to confirm the existence of the 13 oz. ice tea glass in Royal Ruby.

Anchor Hocking produced three types of crystal stemware. There are several differences between the Inspiration, Early American (bubble) on the left, and Berwick (boopie) on the right. The shape of the stem and the number and type of "bumps" on the three bases vary considerably.

Detail of the Inspiration crystal stem. Notice the definite clockwise twist in the design.

Newport

This pattern, often referred to as "Coupe" by collectors, was made in a variety of colors and sizes. Five sizes of glasses and three colors of this pattern were listed in the catalogs. However, Royal Ruby was made but never listed. I have only seen four sizes of this glass in Royal Ruby, with many being marked with the familiar "anchor over H" emblem embedded in the glass. I don't believe the matching pitcher was ever produced in Royal Ruby. Also note the pitcher listed with Newport was also listed with Chateau in the same catalog.

Left to right: 16 oz. iced tea #R3676, 6", $10-15; 12 oz. beverage #R3672, 5", $10-12; 7 oz. juice #R3677, 4", $8-10; 9 oz. on-the-rocks #R3670, 3", $8-10.

Newport 12 oz. beverage #R3672, 5", $20-25. This Lil' Abner glass was sold at Dogpatch U.S.A. Li'l Abner™ was the first comic strip to star mountaineers as main characters. The comic strip, which first appeared in 1934, was the brainchild of Al Capp. Capp's full name was Alfred Gerald Coplin. He was born in New Haven, Connecticut, in 1909 and was the first of four children. Capp mastered every technique postmodernists celebrate: parody, satire, irony, chaos, the surreal, juxtaposition, and the slapstick of differences. Capp created an inverted folk fertility ritual, the Sadie Hawkins Day, which survives today in high schools across the nation. In 1965, Capp cut a deal with Pepsi™ to use the name Mountain Dew™ to describe their new tangy yellow soda and another deal with the National NuGrape Co. of Atlanta to use the name Kickapoo Joy Juice™. These ventures were so successful that Capp, after two decades of withholding merchandising rights from theme parks, finally agreed to license his characters to O.J. Snow, a real estate appraiser and salesman, for a park to be built on 825 acres of land in Marble Falls, Arkansas. Dogpatch was born and the park opened in 1968. The park created quite a bit of controversy. Capp had commented about the Ozarks being "just a notch below a garbage heap." After reading this, Arkansas state officials said Dogpatch would undermine the image of the state and especially the pioneer, the so-called Arkansas hillbilly. The Dogpatch theme park of 1998 is a ragged remnant of its original state. Long gone were the surrey rides, celebrity visits, and live animal shows. Only the glass souvenir picturing Li'l Abner and a few articles in the local newspapers survive to document this unique institution of American Folklore.

Newport 7 oz. juice #R3677 with etching, 4", $10-12.

Newport 12 oz. beverage #R3672 marked with 40th anniversary in 22 kt. gold, 5", $12-15.

Aftermarket candle made with a Newport 12 oz. beverage #R3672, 7" total height, $15-20.

Reunion, Dallas, Texas. Newport 7 oz. juice #R3677, 4", $8-10.

Left to right: Newport 12 oz. beverage #R3672,
5", $10-12; 7 oz. juice #R3677, 4", $8-10.

Newport 12 oz. beverage #R3672 glasses, 5", $10-15 each. Left to right: Oklahoma City Zoo;
Indy 500, Abou Ben Adhen Temple Ron McCormick Potentate 1978; Arkansas Razorback.

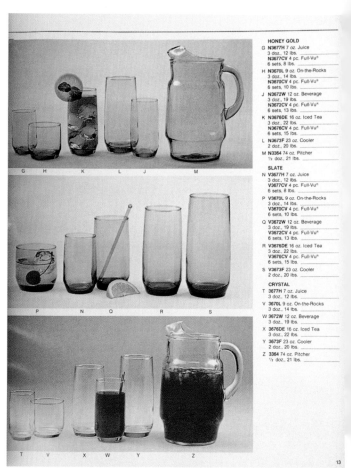

HONEY GOLD
G N3677H 7 oz. Juice
3 doz., 12 lbs.
N3677CV 4 pc. Full-Vu®
6 sets, 8 lbs.
H N3670L 9 oz. On-the-Rocks
3 doz., 14 lbs.
N3670CV 4 pc. Full-Vu®
6 sets, 10 lbs.
J N3672W 12 oz. Beverage
3 doz., 19 lbs.
N3672CV 4 pc. Full-Vu®
6 sets, 13 lbs.
K N3676DE 16 oz. Iced Tea
3 doz., 22 lbs.
N3676CV 4 pc. Full-Vu®
6 sets, 15 lbs.
L N3673F 23 oz. Cooler
2 doz., 20 lbs.
M N3364 74 oz. Pitcher
½ doz., 21 lbs.

SLATE
N V3677H 7 oz. Juice
3 doz., 12 lbs.
V3677CV 4 pc. Full-Vu®
6 sets, 8 lbs.
P V3670L 9 oz. On-the-Rocks
3 doz., 14 lbs.
V3670CV 4 pc. Full-Vu®
6 sets, 10 lbs.
Q V3672W 12 oz. Beverage
3 doz., 19 lbs.
V3672CV 4 pc. Full-Vu®
6 sets, 13 lbs.
R V3676DE 16 oz. Iced Tea
3 doz., 22 lbs.
V3676CV 4 pc. Full-Vu®
6 sets, 15 lbs.
S V3673F 23 oz. Cooler
2 doz., 20 lbs.

CRYSTAL
T 3677H 7 oz. Juice
3 doz., 12 lbs.
V 3670L 9 oz. On-the-Rocks
3 doz., 14 lbs.
W 3672W 12 oz. Beverage
3 doz., 19 lbs.
X 3676DE 16 oz. Iced Tea
3 doz., 22 lbs.
Y 3673F 23 oz. Cooler
2 doz., 20 lbs.
Z 3364 74 oz. Pitcher
½ doz., 21 lbs.

13

Ringling Brothers and Barnum and Bailey glasses. Left to right: 12 oz. beverage #R3672, 5", $15-20; 9 oz. on-the-rocks #R3670, 3", $5-10. Both glasses have a tiger on one side and the picture of the "big top" on the other side.

1978 Anchor Hocking Bulk Catalog page listing the Newport pattern. Notice this pitcher is also used with the Chateau pattern listed earlier in this chapter.

Newport 9 oz. on-the-rocks #R3670, 3", $5-8. Left to right: Sooner Schooner; Pioneer Village; Reno, Nevada; Alaska.

Old Café

Anchor Hocking produced Old Café glassware from 1936 to 1940. Like Coronation, the Royal Ruby coffee cup was sold with a crystal saucer. The 8" footed tray #A977, often called the low candy dish, was sold with a metal handle. The Old Café lamp is reasonably rare and I have not found the vase in Royal Ruby.

The Old Café lamp was made in crystal, pink, and Royal Ruby. The lower edge of the lamp is easily chipped and pristine lamps are reasonably hard to find. Below are the lamps in Royal Ruby, $50-75, and crystal, $25-35.

Closeup of the feet found on the Old Café Lamps. They were added to the vase so the cord could exit the inside of the lamp.

Oyster and Pearl

Oyster and Pearl was produced from 1938 to 1940. The pattern was produced in pink, crystal, Royal Ruby, and white fired on either green or pink. Only items were produced in Royal Ruby. The 5 1/4" heart-shaped, 1-handled bowl and 5 1/2" round, 1-handled bowl are often confused. The heart shaped bowl has a small pour spout on the side opposite the handle. Also, the area where the handle is attached is slightly flattened, giving rise to the "heart shape." I wanted to include a side-by-side photo of the two bowls, however I could not locate the 1-handled, heart shaped bowl in Royal Ruby.

Aftermarket handle added to the 10 1/2" Oyster and Pearl console bowl #A889, $40-55; $10-15 for the handle only.

Provincial

Royal Ruby Provincial, commonly known as "bubble" by collectors, was designated as the R-1600 series that was produced in 1963. The pitcher and glasses were sold in a variety of sets. They were sold in the R1600/55 (9-Piece Refreshment Set), R1600/56 (24-Piece Hostess Service Set), R1600/57 (25-Piece Refreshment Set), R1600/58 (24-Piece Hostess Service Set), and a 15-Piece Refreshment Set. So far, no Royal Ruby sugars or creamers have been found. Most of the Provincial pieces are marked with paper labels. However, I have found the 12 oz. tumbler #R1612, 6 oz. fruit juice #R1606, 8" berry bowl, and 4 1/2" dessert bowl #R1664 with the "anchor over H" emblem embedded in the glass. The unusual two-tiered tidbits made by Novelty Crystal Corporation were probably given away as premiums for trading stamps during the 1950s. I have tried to confirm this, but have yet to find an old catalog listing these items. Any information would be appreciated.

Three-tier tidbit using the 4 1/2" dessert bowl #R1664, $75-100. This is the only three-tier tidbit I have seen. The bowl is labeled with the "anchor over H emblem."

Two-tier tidbits made with one 8" berry bowl and one 4 1/2" #R1664 dessert bowl, $50-60. Both bowls are marked with the "anchor over H" emblem. The plastic base, crystals separating the bowls, and top were made by Novelty Crystal Corporation, 79-55 Albion Avenue, Elmhurst, New York.

Two-tier tidbits made with one 8" berry bowl and one 4 1/2"
#R1664 dessert bowl, $50-60. Both bowls are marked with
the "anchor over H" emblem. The plastic base, crystals
separating the bowls, and top were made by Novelty Crystal
Corporation, 79-55 Albion Avenue, Elmhurst, New York.
The base is dated 1975 and states "made in Israel."

Two-tier tidbits made with one 8" berry bowl and one 4 1/2"
#R1664 dessert bowl, $50-60. Both bowls are marked with the
"anchor over H" emblem. The plastic base, crystals separating the
bowls, and top were made by Novelty Crystal Corporation, 79-55
Albion Avenue, Elmhurst, New York.

Letter from the Novelty Crystal Corporation indicating the company did not assemble the two-tier tidbits.

16-Piece Provincial Luncheon Set #R1600/59, $150-200. This set consists of four #R1641 dinner plates, four #R1650 cups, four #R1628 saucers, and four #R1664 dessert bowls.

Contents of the 16-Piece Provincial Luncheon Set #R1600/59.
Only the dinner plates were labeled with paper labels.

ew of the 16-piece set so you can see how the items are arranged. oth sets I have were opened from the bottom; therefore, the dinner ates appear first.

The saucers were placed on top of the dinner plates.

he dessert bowls and cups were placed on the top f the set in the box.

R-1700

The R-1700 pattern was produced in the 1940s. Mo of the pieces were marked with paper labels.

50-Piece Set of Royal Ruby #R1700/245, $700-750. All 50 pieces of this set have paper labels.

The shipping label states the set was delivered to the Lehigh Suppl Co., 434 Main Street, Bethlehem, Pennsylvania.

The 50-piece set consists of eight coffee cups #R1779, eight saucers #R1729, eight 6 1/2 oz. sherbets #R3313, eight 6 1/4" sherbet plates #R828, eight dinner plates #R1741, eight 10 oz. goblets #R3316, one creamer #R1754, and one sugar #R1753. You will notice the "flat" sugars and creamers are part of both the 50-piece set and 38-piece set of R-1700. Also, the original factory sheets list the "flat" sugar and creamer as R-1700, not R-4000 as in other colors of glassware.

Bottom layer of the 50-piece set showing the arrangement of the coffee cups and sherbets. The eight saucers are placed vertically on the side of the box.

Middle layer of the 50-piece set showing the arrangement of the dinner plates, sugar, creamer, and sherbet plates.

Top layer of the 50-piece set showing the arrangement of the eight tumblers.

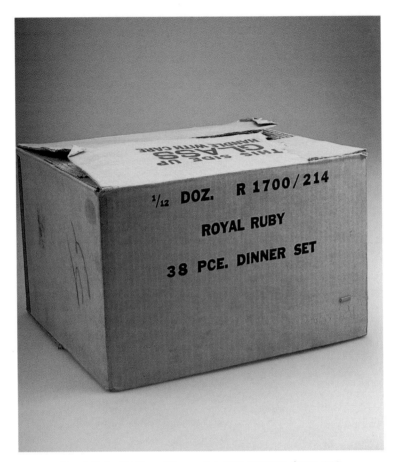

Royal Ruby 38-Piece Dinner Set #R1700/214, $350-450.
All 38 pieces of this set have paper labels.

The 38-Piece Dinner Set consists of six coffee cups #R1779, six saucers #R1729,
six 6 1/2 oz. sherbets #R3313, six 6 1/4" sherbet plates #R828, six dinner plates
#R1741, six 10 oz. goblets #R3316, one creamer #R1754, and one sugar #R1753.

Bottom layer of the 38-Piece Dinner Set. The 10 oz. goblets, creamer, and sugar are located on the bottom layer. The dinner plates, sherbet plates, and saucers are placed vertically along the edges of the box.

Top layer of the 38-Piece Dinner Set. The cups and sherbets make up the top layer of the set.

Dinner plate #R1741 with etched flowers, 9 1/8", $15-20.

Salad plate #R1738 with "INDIANA STATE CAPITAL
INDIANAPOLIS" in 22 kt. gold, 7 3/4", $15-20.

Salad plate #R1738 with "KENTUCKY, THE BLUE GRASS
STATE" in 22 kt. gold, 7 3/4", $15-20.

Roly Poly

This pattern was undoubtedly made for several years. Given the R3600 designation, Roly Poly was sold in at least three different sets: 9-Piece Iced Tea Set #R3600/2, 24-Piece Refreshment Set #R3600/4, and the 19-Piece Refreshment Set #R3600/5. The 1971 catalog lists two other sizes of Roly Poly, the 9 oz. on-the-rocks and the 6 oz. juice. These are listed in crystal in the catalog but they may exist in Royal Ruby.

9 oz. table tumbler #R3651 containing Old Reliable tea bags, 4 1/4", $25-55. The glass contained 16 tea bags made by the Dayton Spice Mills Company.

Finely detailed 9 oz. table tumbler #R3651 with painted grasses and dandelion seed heads, 4 1/4 ", $12-15. The rim of the glass is trimmed in 22 kt. gold.

Closeup of Old Reliable lid.

1950 Flint Glass Union 13 oz. beverage/ice tea #R3658, 5", $12-15.

13 oz. Beverage/ice tea #R3658 embossed with "Tin Type," 5", $20-30.

9 oz. table tumblers #R3651 used by a group of people who met regularly for parties. The glasses were etched with some interesting sayings. Left to right: "Babe & Swell Gal 1952"; "Myrtle from Dorothy & Walt 1950, I hope you choke"; "Dusty's Private Glass – Hands Off! 1950"; "To Bill: my great big hunk of male humanity, love from Mert 1950"; "Mickey's private glass – hands off ! 1952 Use carefully"; and "Joseph 1950."

Commemorative glasses sold by Chapman's Grocery Stores to promote the sale of cottage cheese, 5", 13 oz., $75-80 for the set of four with the lids, $40-50 without the lids.

Closeup of the lid which states "Chapman's Creamed Cottage Cheese, Small Curd, Pasteurized 13 oz. net."

Etched 5 oz. fruit juice #R3653, 3 3/8", $8-10. The etched design is a grape cluster and leaves.

Roly Poly Pitcher and 13 oz. beverage/ice tea #R3658 with etched tulips, $100-125 for the entire set.

Wexford

Wexford is one pattern Anchor Hocking still produces and lists in the 1997 catalog. Many items were made in flashed Wexford. They are not "true" Royal Ruby but actually clear glass sprayed with a red lacquer.

Flashed Wexford votives, $2.

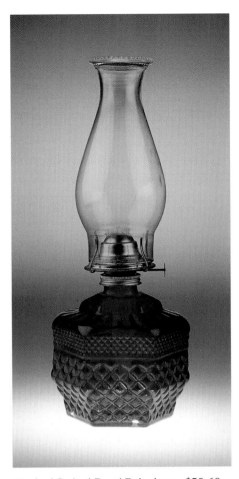

Wexford flashed Royal Ruby lamp, $50-60.

Windsor

Anchor Hocking produced Windsor glassware in the 1940s. The 60 oz. pitcher #A1153, 9 oz. tumbler #A1131, and 5 oz. fruit juice #A1133 are generally found in Royal Ruby. There may be variations in the number of rows of "cubes" on Royal Ruby glasses, since I have found at least three different variations in crystal and light green. Also, I have purchased a light green 4 3/4" 12 oz. tumbler with four rows of "cubes." This is a previously unknown size which may have been produced in Royal Ruby.

Etched 5 oz. fruit juice #A1133, 3 1/4", $10-12.

Several types of bottles are listed in this chapter: water bottles, beer bottles, and liquor bottles. The water bottles are common in crystal, reasonably hard to find in Forest Green, and rare in Royal Ruby. The Royal Ruby beer bottles were manufactured for Schlitz, Pfeiffer, and Rolling Rock breweries.

Nine designs of beer bottles were made for Schlitz. The dates of manufacturing are listed on the bottom of the bottle as a two-digit number. Also, there is the familiar "anchor over H" emblem, the words "Royal Ruby

Anchorglass," and the number 5 to indicate the place of manufacturing (plant 5 in Connellsville, Pennsylvania. Three styles of bottles were marketed in 1949, 1950, and 1963. There were 21 million 32 oz. quart bottles (mold #8585C), 29 million 7 oz. bottles (mold #67-22), and 4 million 12 oz. bottles (mold #168-38B) made. The total production was 100 bottles each of the other six trial styles which were never marketed. Eight of the nine Schlitz bottle designs are pictured in this chapter.

Ribbed water bottle with a chrome plated band and solid maple wood handle, $250-300.

Ribbed water bottle with a chrome plated band and solid maple wood handle, $35-50. This bottle can be found in crystal with relative ease, but it is rare in Royal Ruby.

Did you ever wonder why beer was placed in Royal Ruby bottles? Well beer, like so many other substances, is affected by light and must be protected from the effects of direct light exposure. Ruby red glass absorbs most of the visible spectrum of light. The glass does allow the transmission of the red portion of the visible spectrum, but this portion contains the least energy. By absorbing the majority of the energy of the visible spectrum, red glass protects the beer and greatly extends the beer's "shelf life." During the development of Royal Ruby beer bottles, plant employees placed full bottles of beer in red bottles on the roof of the plant during the summer in direct sunlight. With temperatures reaching over 100 degrees Fahrenheit and the bottles in direct sunlight all day long, the beer should have "spoiled." To everyone's amazement, the beer was still good after two weeks on the roof. Now, why isn't beer still bottled in red? The production costs of Royal Ruby beer bottles was prohibitive and beer drinkers did not readily accept beer in red bottles. The red bottles were an expensive novelty that soon disappeared.

Another question pops up at this point. If the company was making other bottles like the twist off tops, why didn't they produce the bottles for another company? I was told by a company executive that Schlitz threatened legal action if the Royal Ruby bottles were made for another brewer. In essence, the Royal Ruby bottles were a "trademark" for Schlitz and Schlitz wasn't going to allow another company to use their trademark red bottle. Anchor Hocking had already produced several million experimental "twist off" bottles. With legal action looming on the horizon, the decision was made to cease the development and production of new Royal Ruby beer bottles and destroy all those that were awaiting shipment. Since the red glass could not be reused, because additional heating would cause the color to turn to brown, the bottles were crushed and buried. Few examples of these experimental bottles exist today.

beer bottle made in 1941, mold #8569, $40-50.

Left to right: slim select beer bottle, mold #67-37, $75-80; select beer sample bottle, mold #8589, $100-110. These bottles only differ slightly in the style of the closure. Both bottles were made at plant 5 (Connellsville, Pennsylvania) in 1949. There is the familiar "anchor over H" emblem and words "Royal Ruby Anchorglass" on the bottom of both designs. The #67-37 select beer bottle was an experimental design produced for Schlitz. Less than 100 of these bottles were produced.

Beer bottle, mold #61-38, $100-110. This bottle, made in 1949 at plant 5, has a knurled surface and the shoulder states, "NOT TO BE REFILLED – NO DEPOSIT NO RETURN."

Knurled bottles have numerous small ridges or bumps on the surface. This bottle was an experimental design produced for Schlitz. Less than 100 of these bottles were produced.

Rare sample beer bottle, mold #8562, $100-110. The bottle, made in 1947 plant 2, is not knurled and the shoulder states, "NOT TO BE REFILLED - NO DEPOSIT NO RETURN."

Left to right: export beer bottle with smooth surface, mold #63-38A, $100-110; export beer bottle with knurled surface, mold #63-38B, $50-60; export beer bottle with a knurled surface, mold #63-38C, $50-60. The #63-38A export beer bottle was an experimental design produced for Schlitz. Less than 100 of these bottles were produced.

The seven sizes of juice bottles, made in 1949 or 1950 at plant 5, came in two distinct closure designs. One style used a twist off cap while the other used a snap lid. Both versions of the closure are seen here. Left to right: mold #50-76A, finish 28-400 (snap cap), 9 1/2", $40-50; mold #50-64A, finish 27-870 (screw cap), 8 1/2", $40-45; mold #50-51A, finish 28-400 (snap cap), 7 1/4", $35-40; mold #50-40, finish 27-870 (screw cap), 6 5/8", $35-40; mold #50-28, finish 27-870 (screw cap), 5 3/4", $35-40; mold #50-21, finish 27-870 (screw cap), 5 1/2", $35-40; mold #50-14, finish 27-870 (screw cap), 4 3/4", $15-20.

Closeup of the snap cap for the juice bottles. This is called finish #28-400.

Closeup of the screw cap for the juice bottles. This is called finish #27-870.

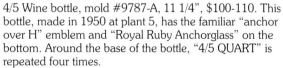

4/5 Wine bottle, mold #9787-A, 11 1/4", $100-110. This bottle, made in 1950 at plant 5, has the familiar "anchor over H" emblem and "Royal Ruby Anchorglass" on the bottom. Around the base of the bottle, "4/5 QUART" is repeated four times.

Liquor bottle, mold #9783-B, 10", $100-110. This bottle, made in 1950 at plant 5, has the familiar "anchor over H" emblem and "Royal Ruby Anchorglass" on the bottom. Around the base of the bottle, "4/5 QUART" is repeated four times. The shoulder of the bottle states, "FEDERAL LAW FORBIDS SALE OR RE-USE OF THIS BOTTLE."

Baby food jar, 3 1/2", $25-30. Only "Royal Ruby Anchorglass" is written on the bottom of the bottle.

Squatty beer bottle, mold #63-22, 6 3/4", $40-50. This bottle, made in 1950 at plant 5, has the familiar "anchor over H" emblem and "Royal Ruby Anchorglass" on the bottom. The shoulder of the bottle states, "NO DEPOSIT NO RETURN – NOT TO BE REFILLED."

Chili sauce bottle, mold #52-33, 6 7/8", $65-75. This bottle, made in 1950 at plant 5, has the familiar "anchor over H" emblem and "Royal Ruby Anchorglass" on the bottom.

Ketchup bottle, mold #9547, 8 1/4",
$75-85. This bottle, made in 1950 at
plant 5, has the familiar "anchor over
H" emblem and "Royal Ruby
Anchorglass" on the bottom.

Sample beer bottle, mold #B33246-X,
10 1/4", $125-135. This bottle, made in
1963 at plant 5, has the familiar "anchor
over H" emblem and "Royal Ruby" on the
bottom. The shoulder states, "NOT TO BE
REFILLED – NO DEPOSIT*NO RETURN."

Aspirin bottle, mold #82-15A, 4 1/2", $15-20.
This bottle, made at plant 5, has the familiar
"anchor over H" emblem and "Royal Ruby
Anchorglass" on the bottom.

Scarce beer bottle, mold #8580, 7", $100-125. This bottle, made in 1947 at plant 2, has the familiar "anchor over H" emblem on the bottom. The shoulder states, "NOT TO BE REFILLED – NO DEPOSIT NO RETURN." Only the bottom of the bottle has been knurled.

32 oz. Schlitz Beer bottle, mold #8585C, 9 1/2", $85-100 with the labels, $20-25 without the labels. Anchor Hocking produced approximately 21 million of these bottles. However, this is the only example I have seen with the original Schlitz labels in place.

Left to right: rare Rolling Rock 7 oz. beer bottle in Royal Ruby, 4 7/8", $250-275; 12 oz. Rolling Rock beer bottle in green, 6", $5-8; 7 oz. Rolling Rock beer bottle in green, 5 1/8", $5-8. The plaster horse in the background was located at a flea market in Ohio.

Whiskey bottle, 7 1/2", $150-200. This bottle, made in 1950 at plant 13, has the familiar "anchor over H" emblem and "Royal Ruby Anchorglass" on the bottom. The back of the bottle states, "FEDERAL LAW FORBIDS SALE OR RE-USE OF THIS BOTTLE."

Beer bottle, mold #8565A, 6 3/4", $100-110. This bottle, made in 1949 at plant 5, has the familiar "anchor over H" emblem and "Royal Ruby Anchorglass" on the bottom. The shoulder states, ."NOT TO BE REFILLED – NO DEPOSIT NO RETURN." The knurling extends to the top of the bottle. The #8565A beer bottle was an experimental design produced for Schlitz. Less than 100 of these bottles were produced.

16 oz. Beer bottle, mold #168-50, 7 3/8", $100-110. This bottle, made in 1963 at plant 5, has "Royal Ruby" on the bottom. The shoulder states, "NOT TO BE REFILLED – NO DEPOSIT*NO RETURN." The #168-50 beer bottle was an experimental design produced for Schlitz. Less than 100 of these bottles were produced.

Mayonnaise jar, mold #10-51, 5 1/8", $100-125. The bottom of the bottle has the familiar "anchor over H" emblem.

Flashed whiskey bottle, mold #63-75, 10 3/4", $100-125. Only 34 of the flashed bottles were made. This bottle, made in 1954 at plant 5, has the familiar "anchor over H" emblem on the bottom. The shoulder states, "NOT TO BE REFILLED – NO DEPOSIT*NO RETURN."

Throw away beer bottle, mold #168-38B, 5 3/4", $30-40. This bottle, made in 1963 at plant 5, has the familiar "anchor over H" emblem and "Royal Ruby" on the bottom. The shoulder states, "NOT TO BE REFILLED – NO DEPOSIT*NO RETURN." Anchor Hocking produced approximately 4 million of these bottles.

Beer bottle, mold #8568, 6 1/4", $125-135. This bottle, made in 1947 at plant 2, has the familiar "anchor over H" emblem on the bottom. The shoulder states, "NOT TO BE REFILLED – NO DEPOSIT NO RETURN."

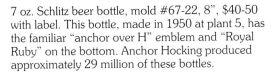

7 oz. Schlitz beer bottle, mold #67-22, 8", $40-50 with label. This bottle, made in 1950 at plant 5, has the familiar "anchor over H" emblem and "Royal Ruby" on the bottom. Anchor Hocking produced approximately 29 million of these bottles.

Front and back view of the rare Owl bank, 7", $250-300. Only about two dozen of these banks were produced and many of those were damaged when large coins were dropped into the bank causing the bottom to either crack or fall out.

Chapter Three
Apothecary/Candy Jars

Anchor Hocking marketed six styles of candy and apothecary jars. At least the three styles were made in Royal Ruby. The 22 oz. stemmed candy jar was made in Forest Green, but the color of the jar was "flashed" or applied as a coating. The "flashing" is not part of the glass and will flake off over time.

The 10 oz. stemmed candy jar with intricate etching, $20-25. The etching contains music notes and a sentimental dedication "To Ethyl."

Left to right: unusual ruby flashed 10 oz. stemmed candy jar, $20-30; 10 oz. stemmed candy jar which contained bath oil pearls, $20-25.

24 oz. Candy jar with The University of the Pacific in 22 kt. gold, 8 1/2", $15-20.

Chapter Four
Ash Trays

Anchor Hocking catalogs list over 25 types and styles of ash trays. They were made in crystal, avocado, honey gold, milk white, Forest Green, and Royal Ruby. I have found the "anchor over H" emblem embedded in the glass on only some of the 5 3/4", 4 5/8", and 3 1/2" square ash trays. The mark is located in one corner of the base.

Closeup of three footed ashtray, 4", $5-8.

The 5 3/4" #R32 ashtray mounted on a cast metal pedestal, $15-20.

Dean Mogle and "Nor-So Camden Arkansas"

Dean Mogle was an Arkansas artist that began his artistic career at Carmark Pottery Company in Camden, Arkansas. After the company closed, Dean opened his own art studio in Camden and began decorating Anchor Hocking glassware. He decorated Royal Ruby, Milk White, Lace Edge, White Swirl, Golden Shell, Golden Anniversary, Hobnail, Vintage, and an assortment of ashtrays, beverage glasses, and crystal items. Not all his work is marked with the "Nor-So Camden Arkansas" emblem. Much of his work involved 22 kt. gold decorations and he was known for his unusual "sponge painting" technique. Dean sold much of his work as he drove around the Ozarks in his Mercury automobile. Much of his limited production of decorated items was sold to local stores, gift shops, and souvenir stands. The studio was closed in 1964 and Dean Mogle passed away in 1976.

5 3/4" Ash tray #R32 decorated by Dean Mogle at his Nor-So Custom Art Studio, $40-50. The ashtray has been "sponge" painted with 22 kt. gold. *Ash tray courtesy of Dr. Leonette Walls.*

Not all pieces Dean Mogle painted had this familiar mark.

Many of the pitchers and glasses included in this chapter have also been listed under the specific pattern. This was done to make this book more "user friendly." I have also included many novelty tumblers, since they are interesting to collect and often provide dates useful in determining when certain patterns were produced. I have included some new pattern names such as Newport and Chateau. Many of these patterns are listed in later catalogs issued after the company stopped producing Royal Ruby. Also, many of the glasses, such as the Savoy pattern, were made for restaurants and are listed only in the institutional glassware catalogs.

Original factory sheet listing the #R3555 footed goblet. Notice the #R3555 tumbler was stamped with "Discontinued."

13 oz. Savoy goblet made for restaurants, 6 1/2", $15-20.

10 1/2 oz. Footed goblet #R3555, 5 1/4", $15-20. The original factory advertising sheet lists this glass as discontinued. However, some glasses were made in limited numbers.

Most of Anchor Hocking's dual colored stemmed glasses were made by joining the stem and bowl (made separately) together with a "wafer" of hot glass. The company experimented with some one-piece Royal Ruby stemmed glasses. However, the stems were very thin and the majority of the glasses broke during production. Production of these "one-piece" glasses was very limited and few of the glasses survive today. Left to right: 5 1/2 oz. glass, 8 5/8", $15-20; 12 oz. glass, 8", $15-20; 10 oz. glass, 7 1/8", $15-20.

4 1/2 oz. Savoy goblet made for restaurants, 5 3/8", $12-15.

Straight shells. Left to right: 16 oz. Gazelle long boy ice tea, 6 1/2 ", $12-15; 12 oz. plain shell, 6 1/4", $20-25; 12 oz. shell with enameled designs and 22 kt. gold lines, 6 1/4", $20-25; 9 oz. water tumbler #R3509, 4", $20-25. With the exception of the Gazelle long boy ice tea, the other three glasses are relatively rare.

TABLE TUMBLERS - WATER PITCHERS
EVERYDAY SELLERS

631 — 9 oz.
TABLE TUMBLER
Packs 12 doz.—59#

3538 — 9½ oz.
TABLE TUMBLER
Packs 6 doz.—35#

1154 — 9 oz.
BARREL TUMBLER
Packs 6 doz.—44#

1201 — 9 oz.
TABLE TUMBLER
Packs 12 doz.—63#

3509 — 9 oz.
WATER TUMBLER
Packs 12 doz.—48#

3361 — 9 oz.
TABLE TUMBLER
Packs 12 doz.—49#

638 — 12 oz.
ICED TEA
Packs 6 doz.—46#

687 — 80 oz.
ICE LIP PITCHER—BLOWN
Packs 1 doz.—39#

1287 — 80 oz.
ICE LIP PITCHER—BLOWN
Packs 1 doz.—39#

FEATURE DISPLAYS MELT AWAY

1952 Catalog page listing the 9 oz. water tumbler.

GOLD BAND and HAIRLINE

A Most Popular Shape

The biggest-looking blown tumbler available in the market.

Supplied in a complete line from Whiskey Glasses to Iced Teas.

Blown; highly polished crystal; with reinforced edge to prevent chipping.

3320/12—1½ OZ. BLOWN
WHISKEY
Pkd. 12 doz.—22 lbs.

3322/12—3 OZ. BLOWN
WINE
Pkd. 12 doz.—22 lbs.

3323/12—5 OZ. BLOWN
FRUIT JUICE
Pkd. 12 doz.—34 lbs.

3321/12—9 OZ. BLOWN
TABLE TUMBLER
Pkd. 12 doz.—50 lbs.

3328/12—12 OZ. BLOWN
ICED TEA
Pkd. 6 doz.—28 lbs.

Catalog page listing all five sizes of the flared tumblers.

Anchor Hocking produced five sizes of these flared tumblers beginning in 1938 with gold lined tumblers in crystal. I have only found four sizes of the glasses, and three sizes exist in Royal Ruby. Left to right: 13 oz. ice tea with enameled lines #R3328, 5 3/4", $20-25; 13 oz. plain ice tea #R3328, 5 3/4", $20-25; 9 1/2 oz. tall tumbler #R3321, 4 5/8", $12-15; 5 oz. fruit juice (#R3323 in Royal Ruby); 3 oz. wine, 3 1/8".

Left to right: 7 oz. old fashioned #R727, 3 3/8", $20-25;
5 oz. old fashioned #R755, 3 1/8", $12-15.

The 10 1/2 oz. goblet #2221 is usually found in crystal.
However, a few were made with Royal Ruby stems. Left to right:
10 1/2 oz. goblet #R2221, 5 1/4", $20-25; 10 1/2 oz. "89er Inn"
goblet #2221, 5 1/4", $5-8.

1967 Anchor Hocking Institutional Catalog listing the #2221
goblet. The other goblets may also exist with Royal Ruby stems.

Left to right: 10 oz. restaurant glass with Royal Ruby stem, 5 3/4", $20-25; 5 oz. restaurant glass with Honey Gold stem, 5", $10-12. This style of glass can also be found with crystal stems and in a variety of sizes.

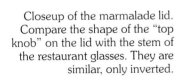

Closeup of the marmalade lid. Compare the shape of the "top knob" on the lid with the stem of the restaurant glasses. They are similar, only inverted.

Etched 2 1/2 oz. footed wine glass #R1755, 3 3/8", 15-20. The etched design is a grape cluster and leaves.

Paper carrier which held four 4 3/4", 9 1/2 oz. tall tumblers #R3597, $20-30.

Plain whiskey #R1506, 1 oz., 3", $10-12.

Etched 42 oz. tilt pitcher, $30-40. This pitcher has an etched design which does differ slightly from the other etched pitcher shown.

Etched 42 oz. tilt pitcher, $30-40.

Metal stemmed glasses. The bowls of these glasses were made by Anchor Hocking, but only for a short period of time. The screw-in portion broke off easily, so production was stopped. Other companies made similar bowls, but the screw-in portions of their bowls show a definite amberina/orange tint.

Closeup of the Anchor Hocking bowl showing the absence of any amberina/orange tinting.

Early American 10 oz. goblet #R336 from the Gordon Lodge, 5 1/4", $15-20.

Boxed set of eight 16 oz. gold leaf tumblers #R400/80-GOLD, 5 3/4", $60-75.

Etched gold band and hairline tumblers, 4 3/4", $30-40 for the set of six tumblers. There are two of each of the following inscriptions: "Violet Johnson 1943"; "Mom and Doc compliments of Violet, Emery, Art 1943"; "To Doc & Naomi from Gladys & Elenore 1943."

The majority of the relish trays/lazy susans were not sold by Anchor Hocking. They were included in the book because the trays used Old Café inserts. The crystal, Forest Green, and Royal Ruby inserts are interchangeable in the trays. The unlined inserts were used in a silver plated tray made by Sheridan Silver Company. While Royal Ruby Old Café glassware is not extremely abundant, the relish tray inserts must have been made in great quantity.

Anchor Hocking made four different relish tray inserts: Forest Green, $8-10; Royal Ruby, $8-10; crystal with lines on the bottom, $5-8; crystal with no lines on the bottom, $5-8.

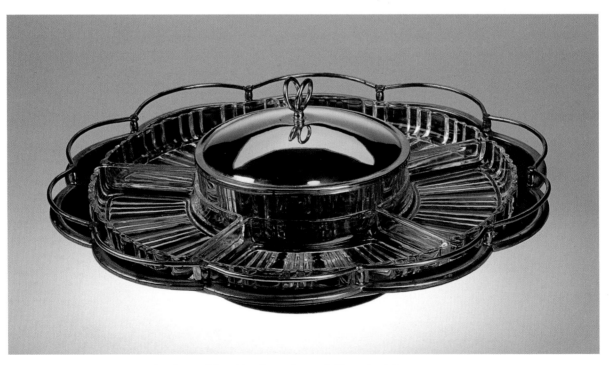

Art deco relish set (maker unknown). The set rotates on a metal base attached to the tray. The complete set, $50-75.

Throughout the period of 1940 to 1964, Anchor Hocking made countless novelties in Royal Ruby. Very few were trademarked in the glass. The majority of the pieces were marked with paper labels. Also included in this chapter are items which didn't seem to fit in any other chapter.

Relish dish with metal handle, 4 1/2" x 6", $15-20.

Crystal marmalade jar with Royal Ruby cover #E514, $20-30. This version has 22 kt. gold lines painted on the lid.

Closeup of the brass filigree.

Unusual saucer with both brass filigree edging
around the plate and a brass handle, $25-30.

Metal swan centerpiece which uses the #765/205 flower basket and block. This
bowl has closed handles and three projections on the inside surface for the flower
block to rest on. Notice the scallops on the upper edge of the bowl. The crystal
candy jar with Royal Ruby cover #E775 will also fit in the centerpiece.

The 1952 catalog lists the #765/205 flower basket
and block.

Crystal candy jar with Royal Ruby cover #E775, 5 1/2", $15-20.

Closeup of the upper edge of the bowl. Notice this edge is flat, while the other two versions of this bowl have scalloped edges. Also note the absence of the flower block supports.

Closeup of the handle of the #E775 candy jar. Notice the handle is open.

Gold plated candy jar, 5 1/2", $12-15. This dish is hard to find with the 22 kt. gold in good condition. This dish, unlike the #765/205 flower basket, does not have the three projections on the inside surface to support the flower block. The upper edge of the bowl is scalloped. There is a third version of this bowl used with the #E775 crystal candy jar with Royal Ruby cover. This bowl has a flat upper edge, no projections to support the flower block, and open handles.

Cigarette box with an etched horse, $80-100. The cover has been partially removed to show the partition on the inside and the ribs on the bottom surface.

Cigarette box with enameled flowers and 22 kt. gold on the lid, $90-100.

Cigarette box with etched deer, $80-100.

Cigarette box with etched flowers, $80-100.

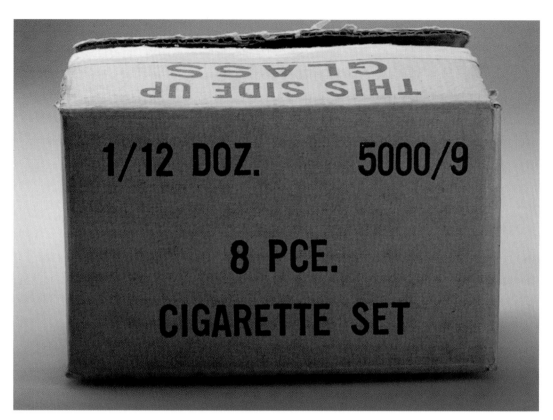

8-piece cigarette set #5000/9, $125-150. $15-20 for the box only.

Overhead view of the 8-piece cigarette set #5000/9. You can see how the crystal cigarette box base, Royal Ruby lid, and six ashtrays are arranged.

Round snack plate, 8 1/8", $40-50 for one plate with the 6 oz. punch cup #R279 (not shown).

Eagle jar reportedly made by Anchor Hocking, 10", $35-50. I have also been told that this jar may be a sales premium given by Wheaton Glass. More research will solve the mystery.

Chip and dip set made with one 8" large bowl #R1078, one 4 1/2" dessert bowl #R1074 bowl, and a brass plated bracket, $25-35.

Rare box of 12 Dietz FITZALL ruby lantern lenses complete with paper labels, $300-350. Box only, $50-75. The use of an Anchor Hocking inventory number in the description of the lenses and the presence of the Anchor Hocking shipping computer punch card on the box with the Dietz name confirms Anchor Hocking did make many, if not most of the red-colored lantern lenses. Note Dietz uses the #R852 number in the description. This is a typical Anchor Hocking item description format.

Closeup of the other side of the Dietz box.

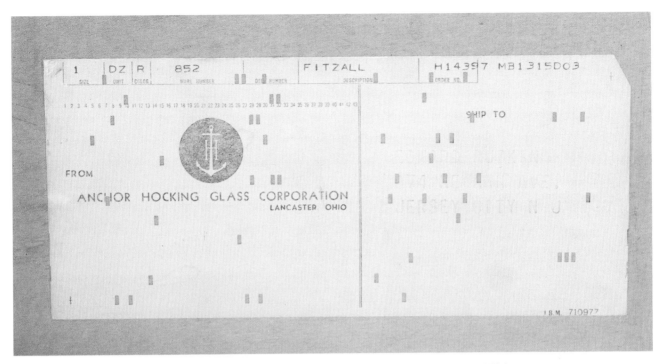

Closeup of shipping punch card from Anchor Hocking. The FITZALL #R852 lenses were delivered to Edward Ruskin, 274 Newark Avenue, Jersey City, New Jersey.

Overhead view showing one dozen Dietz lenses.

Closeup of Dietz paper label.

Dietz FITZALL lantern lens with paper label, 6", $20-25. The company also sold the same lens with lock-knobs to secure the lens in the lantern. These lenses are marked with "DIETZ SYRACUSE, N.Y., U.S.A. FITZALL LOC-NOB REG'D. U.S. PAT. OFF." raised in the glass and were sold without paper labels.

Unfortunately, the box of Dietz LITTLE WIZARD lenses lay in a barn for over twenty years and the box virtually disintegrated. I was able to save the two sides with the markings. The markings are, "ONE DOZEN R851 DIETZ LITTLE WIZARD GLOBES, SYRACUSE, N.Y., U.S.A., RUBY."

The other side of the Dietz LITTLE WIZARD lantern lens box.

Closeup of Dietz paper label. Notice this label has the same basic design and wording as the FITZALL label, but it is red in color instead of blue.

Dietz LITTLE WIZARD lantern lens with paper label, 3 7/8", $20-25.

8-Piece Serva-Snack set #200/42, $25-35.

Overhead view of the 8-Piece Serva-Snack set #200/42 with four Royal Ruby cups and four crystal trays, $25-35. The trays were stacked on the bottom of the box, with the cups arranged as shown.

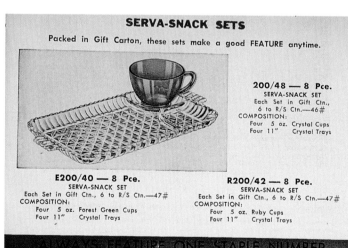

SERVA-SNACK SETS

Packed in Gift Carton, these sets make a good FEATURE anytime.

200/48 — 8 Pce.
SERVA-SNACK SET
Each Set in Gift Ctn.,
6 to R/S Ctn.—46#
COMPOSITION:
Four 5 oz. Crystal Cups
Four 11" Crystal Trays

E200/40 — 8 Pce.
SERVA-SNACK SET
Each Set in Gift Ctn., 6 to R/S Ctn.—47#
COMPOSITION:
Four 5 oz. Forest Green Cups
Four 11" Crystal Trays

R200/42 — 8 Pce.
SERVA-SNACK SET
Each Set in Gift Ctn., 6 to R/S Ctn.—47#
COMPOSITION:
Four 5 oz. Ruby Cups
Four 11" Crystal Trays

ALWAYS FEATURE ONE STAPLE NUMBER

1952 Catalog page listing the Serva-Snack set in crystal with either crystal, Forest Green, or Royal Ruby cups.

Extremely rare Royal Ruby serving platter, 6" by 10", $200-225.

Chapter Eight
Vases

Over the years, Anchor Hocking produced a variety of vases. Most of the vases were trademarked with paper labels. The only vases I have found trademarked with the "anchor over H" emblem embedded in the glass are the crimped top vase #R3306, crimped bud vase #R3303, and the Rainflower vase. The trademark on the Rainflower vase is extremely hard to see, but it can be found with a magnifying glass.

Many of the vases were sold to other companies where they were etched with flowers or figures. The etching process required the piece to be first coated with paraffin wax. The design was then scraped into the wax and the piece subjected to a hydrofluoric acid mist or vapor. The acid dissolved the glass in areas not protected by the wax. After the piece was washed to remove the acid, the paraffin wax was melted off. This left the design, in white, on the surface of the glass.

The 4" ivy ball #R3354 and 6 3/8" vase #R3346 were used to market mosquito repellent candles. Although only one candle is pictured, there are undoubtedly numerous other companies that made the candles. The 4" ivy ball #R3354 can be found in a variety of wall hangers. I have seen many different styles over the years, but only included a couple in the book.

9" Vase #R53 painted with a scene of Niagra Falls. The vase is also marked with "Souvenir of Niagra Falls", $40-50.

Jadeite plate with a painted scene of Niagra Falls, $20-25. Evidently, the same person who painted the vase also painted the plate. Undoubtedly, there are other pieces painted with the same scene.

9" Vase #R53 encased in a basket. I was told the basket was woven by
Native Americans from Maine with reeds growing in the state, $90-100.

Closeup of the neck of the 9" vase encased in the basket.

9" Vase #R53 with etched deer and pine trees. Most of the etched Royal Ruby pieces I have obtained came from Canada. I was told a Canadian company did the etching, but I have been unable to determine the company's name.

9" Vase #R53 with a sterling silver overlay picturing a peacock sitting in a tree, $90-100.

9" Vase #R53 with etched flowers, $40-50.

Left to right: crimped bud vase #R3303 coated with sea shells from Florida. The vase is marked with the "anchor over H" emblem, $20-25; plain crimped bud vase #R3303 with both the paper label and "anchor over H" emblem, $20-25.

Aftermarket creation containing the 4" and 6" scalloped ivy balls in a wrought iron holder. Maker of the holder is unknown, $30-40.

4" Ivy ball in a silver painted holder.
Maker of the holder is unknown, $12-15.

4" Ivy ball in a white painted holder.
Maker of the holder is unknown, $12-15.

4" Ivy ball with *etched flowers*, $12-15.

4" Ivy ball with painted flowers, $12-15.

Two 4" ivy balls with hand painted 22 kt. gold lines and enameled flowers, $15-20 each.

Box of two 4" ivy balls used for Moskeeto Lite insect repellant candles, $25-35.

The top reads: "Moskeeto Lites, Victrylite Candle Co. Oshkosh Wis, Net weight min. 10 oz. Active ingredients per weight 7% 2-phenyl cyclohexanol, 9% 2-cyclohexyl cyclohexanol, vapor booster saturated with 1.5 grams cyclohexyl cyclohexanol, 3.5 grams 2-phenyl cyclohexanol, inert ingredients 90% scented paraffin waxes, direction for use on the box."

4" Ivy ball mounted in a gold painted metal wall hanger. Maker of the hanger is unknown, $12-15.

4" Ivy ball in a gold painted support with leaves.

6" Ivy ball mounted in a white painted metal wall hanger. Maker of the hanger is unknown, $10-15.

Left to right: 6 3/8" vase #R3345 with etched flowers, $15-20; 6 3/8" vase #R3345 which has been diamond cut, $25-35; 6 3/8" vase #R3345 with etched tulips, $15-20.

6 3/8" Vase #R3345 given away as a promotional item for Hart's Grocery in Rochester, New York. This is the original vase and paper bag the vase was wrapped in, $25-35 for both.

6 3/8" Vase #R3345 decorated by the Gay Fad Studios, Lancaster, Ohio, $30-40. Most of these vases were painted and made into lamps.

Chapter Nine

Avon

Small booklet included in some of the Avon Cape Cod items.

Over the years I have wondered if Avon Cape Cod and other ruby red cologne bottles sold by Avon were produced by Anchor Hocking. Two former employees of the company, each with over 35 years at Anchor Hocking, said the company did produce the majority of each item of Avon Cape Cod and all of the other Avon red glass. Wheaton Glass Company also made a limited amount of the Cape Cod pattern and Fostoria is listed as making some of the sales premium items. Four items were not included in the listing for Cape Cod. The pie server was not included because the red handle is plastic, the condiment dish and pedestal mugs were not available in time to be photographed, and the cream pitcher candle is nothing more than the creamer with wax poured inside to create a candle. The items of Avon Cape Cod are listed in the order they were issued beginning with 1975.

For fifteen years the magnificent Avon 1876 Cape Cod Collection has captured the spirit, enthusiasm and superb craftsmanship of a true American original. Our "1990 series" continues in that tradition by celebrating with this beautiful new addition to the line.

Glassmaking began in the United States with the first colonists in 17th century Jamestown, Virginia. By the next century, several glasshouses had been established in Philadelphia, southern New Jersey, Ohio and New York. The workmen were mainly English and German immigrants who drew on the wealth of European glassmaking techniques.

The 19th century saw the number of glasshouses grow from a dozen to nearly one hundred. Machines for pressing glass were constructed in Boston and Cape Cod. The exceptional glass produced by the Boston & Sandwich Glass Works of Cape Cod in particular was the inspiration for the name of this collection.

Avon continues this American tradition by entrusting the production of this fine collection to the Wheaton Glass Company of New Jersey. Wheaton, a family owned and operated business for over a century, has been manufacturing the Cape Cod Collection since 1975.

The Cape Cod Collection is reminiscent of early American "sandwich glass." It recreates the lacy, intricate designs, fine background stippling and expert

Inside the booklet, there is a definite mention of Wheaton Glass making some of the Cape Cod glassware. Anchor Hocking made the majority of the Avon Cape Cod glassware, but a limited production was contracted to Wheaton Glass Company. David Bates, a former employee of Anchor Hocking who was responsible for the "glass batching," said that if a piece was red glass and sold by Avon, Anchor Hocking made it. Paul Stuart, a former employee of Anchor Hocking who worked in the machine shop, also said the company made the Avon Cape Cod glassware.

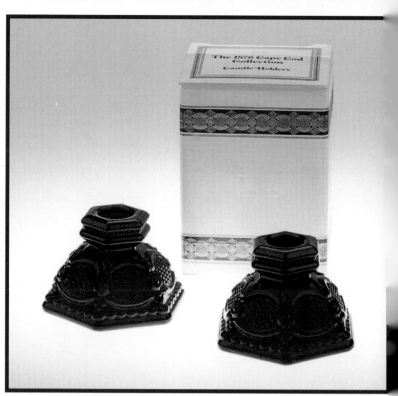

The Candle Holders were issued in 1975 in a box of two, 2 1/2", $15-20 MIB (Mint in Box). The set's issue price was $18.50 for a box of two.

The Cruet was issued in 1975, 6", $10-12 MIB. The cruet's issue price was $11.

The Wine Goblet with Bayberry Fragrance Candlette was issued in 1976, 4 1/2", $10-15. The goblet's issue price was $8.

The Decanter was issued in 1977, 9 3/4", $15-20 MIB. The decanter contained 10 oz. of bubble bath and had an issue price of $20.

The Water Goblet Perfumed Candle Holder was issued in 1977, 6", $15-20 MIB. The goblet's issue price was $11.

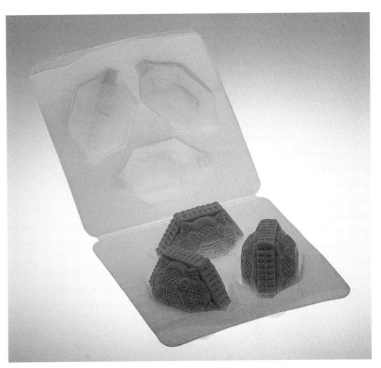

Soap removed from the dessert bowl.

The Dessert Bowl and Three "Special Occasion" Soaps were issued in 1978, 5 1/4", $12-15 MIB. The bowl's issue price was $11.

The Salt Shaker Charisma Cologne with 1.5 fluid oz. was issued in 1978, $10-15 MIB. The shaker's issue price was $6.

The Hostess Bell was issued in 1979, $25-30 MIB. The bell's issue price was $15.

The Dessert Plate was issued in 1980, 7 1/2", $10-12 for a set of two plates MIB. The plate's issue price was $11 for a box of two.

The Sugar Bowl was issued in 1981, $8-10 MIB. The sugar bowl's issue price was $12.

The Water Goblet was issued in 1982, 6", $8-10 MIB. The goblet's issue price was $15.

The Wine Goblet was issued in 1982, 4 1/2", $8-10 MIB. The goblet's issue price was $10.

The Creamer was issued in 1982, $8-10 MIB.
The creamer's issue price was $12.

The Dinner Plate was issued in 1982, 11", $10-15 MIB.
The plate's issue price was $16.

The Dessert Bowl was issued in 1982, 5 1/4", $10-12 MIB.
The bowl's issue price was $12.

The Vase was issued in 1984, 8", $30-35 MIB.
The vase's issue price was $18.50.

The Covered Butter Dish was issued in 1983, 3 1/2" by 7",
$12-15 MIB. The dish's issue price was $18.50.

The Tall Candle Holders were issued in 1983, 8 1/2",
$15-20 MIB. The candle holder's issue price was
$18.50 for two.

The Pitcher was issued in 1985, 48 oz., 8 1/4", $35-45 MIB. The pitcher's issue price was $30.

The Salt and Pepper Shakers were issued in 1984, 4 1/2", $20-25 MIB. The set's issue price was $16.50.

The Hurricane Candle was issued in 1985, 13", $35-40 MIB. The candle's issue price was $25.

The Serving Platter was issued in 1986, 10 3/4" by 13 1/2", $40-50 MIB. The platter's issue price was $29.

The Candy Dish was issued in 1987, 6", $20-25 MIB. The dish's issue price was $21.

The Serving Bowl was issued in 1986, 8 5/8", $20-25 MIB. The bowl's issue price was $19.

The Two Tier Server was issued in 1987, $70-80 MIB. The server's issue price was $37.

The Footed Glass Set was issued in 1988, 3 3/4", $15-20 MIB. The set's issue price was $21.

The Footed Sauce Boat was issued in 1988, $30-40 MIB. The boat's issue price was $31.

The Heart Trinket Box was issued in 1989, $15-20 MIB. The box's issue price was $16.

The Tall Beverage Glass Set was issued in 1990, 5 1/2", $15-20 MIB. The set's issue price was $18.99 for a box of two glasses.

The Napkin Ring Set was issued in 1989, $45-60 MIB. The set's issue price was $25.

The Christmas Ornament was issued in 1990, $15-20 MIB. The ornament's issue price was $9.99.

The Cup/Saucer Set was issued in 1990, $15-20 MIB. The set's issue price was $19.99.

The Saucer Champagne Glass Set was issued in 1991, 5 3/8", $30-35 MIB. The set's issue price was $22.99 for a box of two.

The Pedestal Cake Plate was issued in 1991, 10", $65-70 MIB. The plate's issue price was $49.99.

The Soup/Cereal Bowl was issued in 1991, 7 3/8", $10-12 MIB. The bowl's issue price was $14.99.

The Pie Server Plate was issued in 1992, 11", $25-35 MIB. The plate's issue price was $30.

The Elegant Wine Glass Set was issued in 1992, 5 1/4",
$20-25 MIB. The set's issue price was $14.99.

The Ruby Red Bud Vase which contained 3 oz. of
cologne was issued in 1970-1971, 8 1/4", $10-12
MIB. The cologne's issue price was $5. The bud vase
contained Unforgettable, Rapture, Occur!, Somewhere,
Topaze, or Cotillion cologne.

The Bread and Butter Dish Set was issued in 1992, 5 3/4", $10-15
MIB. The set's issue price was $14.99.

The Candlestick Cologne was issued in 1970-1971, 5 1/4", $10-12 MIB. The cologne's issue price was $6. The candlestick contained Elusive, Charisma, Brocade, Regence, or Bird of Paradise cologne.

The Garnet Bud Vase was issued in 1973-1976, 6 1/2", $5-8 MIB. The vase's issue price was $5. The vase contained "To a Wild Rose" cologne.

The Scent of Roses Decanter contained "Scent of Roses" cologne and was issued in 1972-1973, 4 1/2", $5-8 MIB. The decanter's issue price was $5.

The Strawberry Bath Foam was issued in 1971-1972, 5", $12-15 MIB. The issue price was $4.

Festive Facets Decanter was issued in 1979-1980, $4-5 MIB. The decanter's issue price was $1.50. The decanter came in red, green, and blue glass. A different cologne was packed in each different color of glass, with Charisma coming in the red glass container.

Christmas Bell Decanter similar to the Christmas Song Bell issued in 1975-1976, 5", $10-12.

Unidentified Avon item, 7", $25-30. I have not been able to identify what this item was used for. It appears to be a vase and is clearly marked Avon on the bottom. It was probably a limited edition sales premium.

The Strawberry Bath Gelee was issued in 1971-1972, 3", $8-10 MIB. The original issue price as $7.

Christmas Bells with a silver cap were issued in 1979-1980, 2 1/2", $4-5 MIB. The bell's issue price was $3. The bells originally contained Topaze or Sweet Honesty cologne. The Christmas Bells were first issued in a ruby flashed glass container with a gold cap in 1974-1975.

Chapter Ten
Lamps

Many of the lamps pictured in this chapter were hand painted by the Gay Fad Studios, Lancaster, Ohio. The studio was located near the main plant of Anchor Hocking on West 5th Avenue. It is extremely difficult to find the lamps with the painting intact. The paint was easily removed when rubbed or when subjected to any moisture. The milk glass globes were not securely held in the lamps so they were often broken through the years. Not all the lamps are true Royal Ruby. The 4" and 6" ivy ball varieties were made in flashed versions shown below. Most of the metal parts of the lamps were solid yellow brass. However, I have located three lamps where the metal was brass-plated steel. If the brass needs to be re-plated, the cost of the lamp will escalate considerably. The prices listed below are for complete lamps with pristine paint. When you look through the pictures, note there are different painted flower designs, different base designs, different top designs, and at least four designs of the knobs used to turn on the lamp.

Right: The Old Café lamp was produced in three colors: Royal Ruby, pink, and crystal. Here are the crystal, $25-35, and Royal Ruby lamps, $50-75. The lower edge of the lamps chip easily, so mint condition lamps are uncommon.

Below: Closeup of the "feet," which hold the Old Café lamp up so the electrical cord can exit the lamp.

Early American Prescut Lamp with a Royal Ruby chimney. Sources at the factory said only 6 Royal Ruby chimneys were run one day at the request of the president of the company. The lamps were presented to company officials, $600-650.

Lamp using a 4" ruby flashed ivy ball and milk glass shade, $50-75.

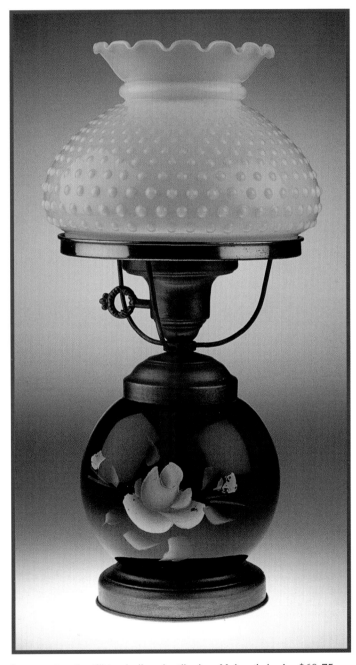

Lamp using the 6" ivy ball and milk glass Hobnail shade, $60-75.

Lamp using the 6" flashed ivy ball and round milk glass shade, $40-50. The glass shade is not well secured in the lamp so it has a tendency to fall and break.

Closeup of the 6" ivy ball showing the cracking that occurs in the flashing as it dries out over the years.

Lamp using the 6" ivy ball and round milk glass shade, $60-75. The glass shade is not well secured in the lamp so it has a tendency to fall and break.

Lamp using the 6" ivy ball and round milk glass shade, $60-75. The glass shade is not well secured in the lamp so it has a tendency to fall and break. This lamp has a different flower than the other 6" ivy ball lamp pictured.

Lamp using the 6 3/8" vase #R3346. This version used a cloth shade that clipped onto the light bulb, $50-60.

Lamp using the 6 3/8" vase #R3346 and round milk glass shade, $60-75. The glass shade that was not well secured in the lamp so it had a tendency to fall and break.

Undecorated lamp using the 9" vase #R53. This version used a cloth shade which clipped onto the wire "harp", $60-75.

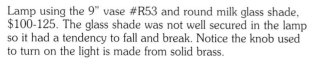

Lamp using the 9" vase #R53 and round milk glass shade, $100-125. The glass shade was not well secured in the lamp so it had a tendency to fall and break. Notice the knob used to turn on the light is made from solid brass.

Closeup of the lamp finial. There is a Royal Ruby marble encased in a solid brass "knob" which is used to secure the shade to the brass wire "harp."

Closeup of the lamp base. There are several styles of lamp bases.

Lamp using the 9" vase #R53. This version used a cloth shade that clipped onto the wire "harp," $80-90 for the complete lamp with top "knob" or finial.

Closeup of the top of the vase. Notice the brass cover completely encases the top of the vase.

Closeup of the top of the vase. Notice the brass cover fits down into the neck of the vase and does not cover up the scalloped top of the vase as in other varieties of the lamp.

Closeup of the lamp base. Compare this to the previous lamp base, they are completely different.

Lamp using the 9" vase #R53 and round milk glass shade, $60-75. The glass shade is not well secured in the lamp so it has a tendency to fall and break. This lamp is painted with a totally different flower design.

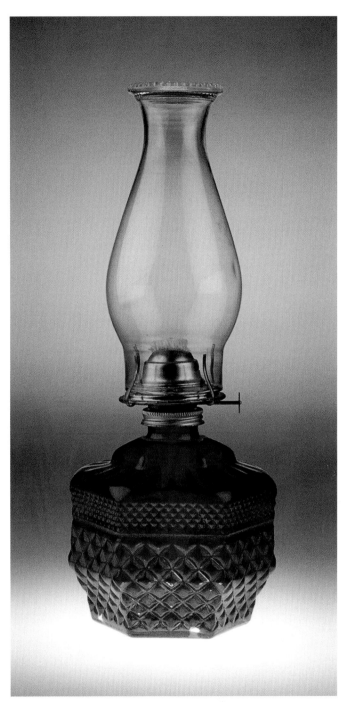

Flashed Forest Green lamp. This lamp was included because it is not made with a vase and the lamp may also exist in Royal Ruby. I have seen the base in flashed Royal Ruby, but at the time I didn't know what is was.

Wexford flashed Royal Ruby lamp, $50-60.

Chapter Eleven
Confusing Similarities

Many items are commonly mistaken for Anchor Hocking's Royal Ruby glassware. Bullseye, made by Wheaton Glass, is often thought of as being made by Anchor Hocking because it was made in a deep red, dark green, light yellow, milk glass, and crystal. These resemble Anchor Hocking's Royal Ruby, Forest Green, Honey Gold, Anchorwhite, and Crystal Clear. A myriad of pieces were produced in the five colors. Glassware produced by Arcoroc of France is also listed as Royal Ruby. This glassware can be found in several sizes of glasses, cup and saucers, and plates. There is another frosted red glassware, maker unknown, which can also be found in several sizes of bowls, cups and saucers, and plates. Remember, Royal Ruby is a trademarked color. Only Anchor Hocking's deep red glassware can be correctly called Royal Ruby.

Bullseye vases in three colors which mimic Anchor Hocking's Royal Ruby, Forest Green, and Honey Gold. I also recently purchased the vase in crystal (not shown).

Bullseye ashtray.

Left to right: Bullseye 7" water glass, syrup dispenser, creamer, and 3 1/2" juice glass.

Left to right: Bullseye vinegar cruet and storage jar.

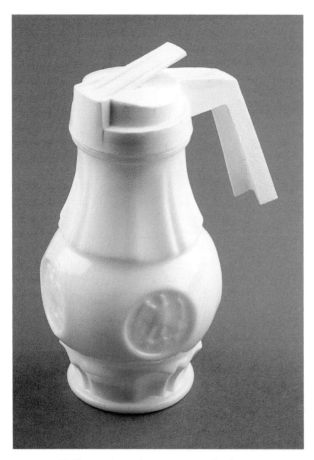

Bullseye syrup dispenser in milk glass.

Ruby red glass made by Arcoroc in France. This glassware is quite common and comes in several sizes of glasses, plates, bowls, cups and saucers. The word "FRANCE" can be found in raised letters on all pieces.

8" Frosted mixing bowl, maker unknown. I have seen this frosted glassware in plates, cups, saucers, and bowls.

Information about the production of Anchor Hocking glassware is limited. I was able to obtain certain advertisement proofs sheets distributed to the magazines. I also included catalog pages to help document Anchor Hocking's glassware production.

Front cover of the *1951 Wards Midsummer Sale Book* .

Listing for Royal Ruby glassware in the *1951 Wards Midsummer Sale Book*

Advertising proof sheet created by Anchor Hocking's Advertising Department.

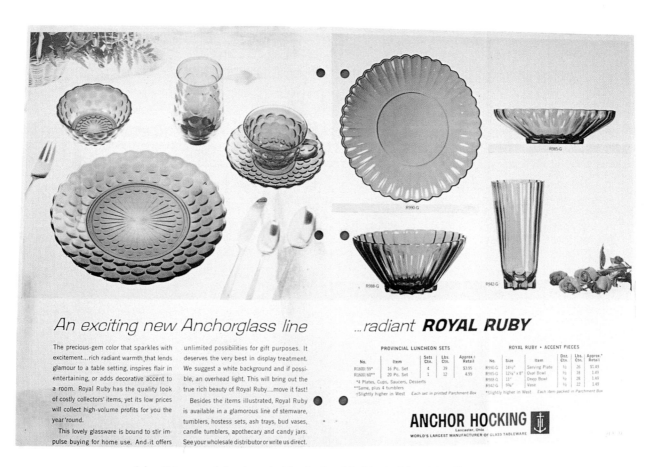

Advertising proof sheet created by Anchor Hocking's Advertising Department.

Advertising proof sheet created by Anchor Hocking's Advertising Department. Even though this does not include Royal Ruby glassware, it is a rare piece of Anchor Hocking documentation. Notice the list of trade publications where the advertisement would appear.

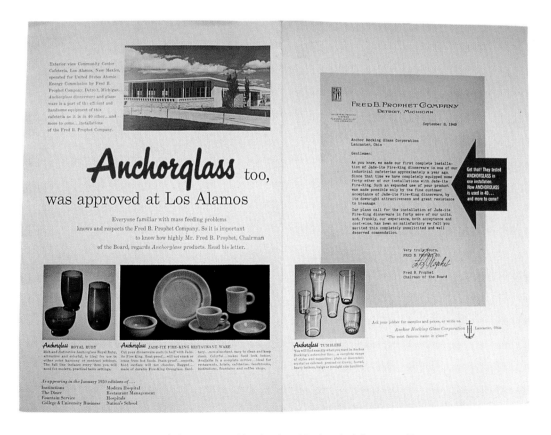

Advertising proof sheet created by Anchor Hocking's Advertising Department.
Notice the list of trade publications where the advertisement would appear.

Advertising proof sheet created by Anchor Hocking's Advertising Department. Even though this does not include Royal Ruby glassware, it is a rare piece of Anchor Hocking documentation. Notice the list of magazines where the advertisement would appear.

The actual advertisement as it appeared in *Good Housekeeping*.

74

Page from the 1964 catalog showing Royal Ruby glassware on display in a store.

---

glassware departments

your high-traffic, high-profit area

More and more retail stores of every type are featuring complete glassware departments — and in many cases, exclusive Anchor Hocking departments. Variety stores and department stores have long departmentalized their glassware, and most super markets have increased the size of their departments. Today, 95% of super markets sell glassware, and 75% have glassware departments. The same trend is dramatically evident in drug chains, hardware and other retail outlets. ▪ Why more glassware departments? Because these high-profit sales areas (40-50% gross) attract traffic year-round and bring additional related sales. ▪ Why Anchor Hocking? No other glassware manufacturer offers such a complete and diversified line of best-selling glass tableware essentials. And you get an extra profit bonus in freight savings through Anchor Hocking's extensive pool car system (see page 77). These, and other reasons, make Anchor Hocking the leading glassware supplier — in supermarkets, for example, preferred over the next six manufacturers combined. ▪ Anchor Hocking merchandising specialists have developed "model" departments for stores of various sizes and types, with recommended balanced stocks of steady-selling staples and best-selling new items. Take advantage of this experience. Anchor Hocking will be happy to supply complete details.

75

Instructions to increase the sales of glassware found in the 1964 catalog.

Chapter Thirteen
What Is It?

Through the years I have accumulated a variety of ruby red items I have been unable to definitively identify. Many of these have the "feel" and color of Anchor Hocking's Royal Ruby. I will offer one free autographed copy of this book to the first person who can identify any of the items shown below. To qualify, I will need a company catalog reference, advertising sheet, or other documentation which, in my opinion, establishes what the item is and who made it. Good luck!

"Grecian" style vases probably made by Wheaton Glass.

Pair of 9 1/2" candlesticks.

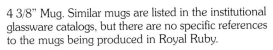
4 3/8" Mug. Similar mugs are listed in the institutional glassware catalogs, but there are no specific references to the mugs being produced in Royal Ruby.

This piece is either one very unusual glass or possibly a vase. I have not seen any item similar in shape or design.

4 1/2" bowl of an unidentified pattern. A crystal relish dish is quite common in this pattern.

Appendix

The information in this appendix appears in *Royal Ruby*, but I think it is helpful to include here as well.

Pricing

The prices in the book are only a guide. They are retail prices for mint condition glassware. Several factors will have an affect on glassware prices: regional availability, depth and consistency in Royal Ruby coloring, the presence or absence of Anchor Hocking markings in the glass or as paper labels, and relative rarity of the piece. Certain items will command higher prices if they are sets in the original packaging. Prices will drop considerably for glassware that is chipped, scratched, cracked, or deformed. No matter what any reference book states, the bottom line is . . .

Glassware is only worth what
someone is willing to pay for it!

Measurements

I have tried to make this reference book as "user friendly" as possible. Too many times I have been in an antiques shop and spotted a tumbler I wanted. The reference book I was using said this was a 12 oz. tumbler. Without a container of liquid and measuring cup I would have no way to actually determine if the tumbler held 12 ounces. I would rather know the tumbler is 5 inches high with a top diameter of 3 inches. This I can measure with a ruler. Unless otherwise noted, the measurements listed in the book are the height of the item. Realize, throughout the production of certain glassware items, the mold dimensions did vary. The measurements in the book are the actual measurements made on the each piece of glassware pictured.

Regional Availability

Over the last seven years I have noticed regional differences in the availability of Royal Ruby glassware. Many items produced by Anchor Hocking were used as promotional items and therefore, were regionally distributed. These items were not listed in the catalog or "jobber" sheets used by sales personnel. For example, the oval vegetable bowl is quite common in the Midwest, but virtually rare on the East Coast. I can go into any antiques mall and see stacks of the bowls. They are usually priced $37.50 and remain on the shelf for months. This local availability will definitely affect pricing!

Resources Available to Collectors

Collectors today have a great variety of resources available. With the advent of the "electronic age," collecting capabilities have been greatly expanded. I can honestly state this book would not have been possible without using the vast resources available, especially on the internet. Below I have listed the resources collectors can use for locating antiques and glassware, however, realize this list is not all inclusive.

Internet Resources

Without leaving the comfort of your home or office, you can search world-wide for items to add to your collection. Presently, there are both antiques dealers and auctions services on the internet.

eBay Auction Service: The eBay Auction Service provides a continually changing source of items. This internet service contains over 750,000 items in 371 categories. Internet users can register as both buyers and/or sellers. The majority of the items remain on the "auction block" for seven days. You can search the auction database for specific items. A list of items will be presented following the search. For example, you might want to find a Fire King Jadite vase made by Anchor Hocking. Because the seller enters the item's description in the database, you often have to anticipate how the item is described. Don't limit the searches. In this case, you might have to search under jadite, hocking, fireking (no space), fire king (with the space), or vase to find the item you want.

Internet Antiques Malls: There are several internet antiques malls I have found to be extremely useful in locating glassware. Each mall contains numerous individual dealers with items for sale. The malls I used are listed below:

• TIAS Mall – (http://www.tias.com/)
• Collector Online Mall – (http:www.collectoronline.com/)
• Facets Mall – (http://www.facets.net/facets/shopindx.htm)
• Depression Era Glass and China Megashow – (http://www.glassshow.com/)
• Cyberattic Antiques and Collectibles – (http://cyberattic.com/)

Glass Shows, Antiques Shops, and Flea Markets: All collectors still enjoy searching the deep dark crevices of the local antiques shops and flea markets. Many of the best "finds" in my personal collection were located in flea markets and "junk" shops. Most of the dealers in glass shows have a good working knowledge of glassware, so "real finds" are not too plentiful.

Periodicals: Both the *Depression Glass Magazine* and *The Daze, Inc.,* are periodicals which will greatly enhance your collecting abilities. Along with the numerous advertisements for glassware, there are informative articles on all facets of collecting glassware.

Websites: (http://home.swbell.net/rrglass/). I have set up a website to convey information about Anchor Hocking glassware. As time goes on, the information will be expanded to include photographs of rare items, unidentified items, and general company information.

Word of Mouth: This is one resource so often overlooked. Let others know what you are looking for. Consider expanding your search by including friends, relatives, and other collectors. This book could not have been written without the help of many fellow collectors.

Do not limit your collecting to only one resource. Remember the items you seek are out there . . . somewhere!

Producing the Royal Ruby Color

Many collectors believe all Royal Ruby glass produced by Anchor Hocking was made using gold to give the glass the familiar deep red color. Many of the pieces made prior to 1950 did contain gold. However, Royal Ruby glass made after that date was made with a glass "batch" mixture containing bismuth, tin, and copper. As the "batch formula" was refined, bismuth was eliminated with no effect on the color. When the Royal Ruby glass was first molded or pressed into shape, it had a very light green color. Once the glass was removed from the molds it was transferred to an annealing oven, called a lehr. The glass was placed in a lehr and the temperature curve adjusted to reheat the glass to 1100 degrees Fahrenheit for 15 minutes. The temperature was reduced gradually over the next 1.5 to 2 hours to anneal, or reduce the internal stresses in the glass. The change from light green to deep red color, termed "striking," occurred during the first 15 to 20 minutes in the lehr. Urea, added to the original glass batch, acted as a reducing agent and changed the glass from a light green to a deep red color.

Most collectors of Royal Ruby glassware have noticed extreme color variations. Some pieces actually have clear areas where the reduction process failed to occur. Three factors affected the "striking" process: temperature, time in the lehr, and the amount of urea in the batch. If the urea level was too low, the glass appeared too light or would not strike. High urea levels caused the ruby color to be too dark. Early lehrs were equipped with asbestos curtains to control the temperature in the striking zone of the annealing process. On some glasses, the thicker bottom areas and rims actually "struck" during the molding process. The first Rainflower vase just came out of the mold and has not turned Royal Ruby. The second Rainflower vase shown here was partially "struck" after being molded and before being put into the lehr. Only the thicker portions remained hot enough before annealing to turn red. If this vase had been placed in the lehr and allowed to reach 1100 degrees Fahrenheit for 15 to 20 minutes, the entire piece would "strike" and would look like the third vase.

Rainflower vase right after being molded.

Rainflower vase partially "struck."

Rainflower vase in Royal Ruby.

Appearance of Markings

Many collectors wonder why the word "Anchorglass" does not appear on pieces of glassware until 1949. As an example, the beer bottle produced for Pfeiffer in 1947 does have the "anchor over H" emblem on the bottom of the bottle, but the word "Anchorglass" is missing. The company applied for numerous trademark patents throughout its long history. The trademark patent for the "anchor over H" emblem was granted in 1938 and the trademark patent for the word "Anchorglass" was granted in 1945. The company began using the "anchor over H" emblem soon after the Hocking Glass Company merged with the Anchor Cap Company in 1937. At that time, they applied for the trademark patent. You will notice the patent application states, "The trademark has been continuously used and applied to said goods in applicant's business since June 11, 1938," while the patent for the word "Anchorglass" does not state the words were already being used.

Registered Apr. 9, 1940   **Trade-Mark 376,781**

UNITED STATES PATENT OFFICE

Anchor Hocking Glass Corporation, Lancaster, Ohio

Act of February 20, 1905

Application November 8, 1938, Serial No. 412,485

STATEMENT

To the Commissioner of Patents:

Anchor Hocking Glass Corporation, a corporation duly organized under the laws of Delaware and located at Lancaster, Ohio, and whose principal place of business is at 109 North Broad Street, Lancaster, Ohio, has adopted and used the trade-mark shown in the accompanying drawing, for GLASS BOTTLES, TUMBLERS, TABLEWARE, CONDIMENT JARS, MIXING BOWLS, AND OTHER FOOD-PREPARING VESSELS, FOOD-PACKING JARS, BOTTLES, JUGS, AND TUMBLERS, COSMETIC JARS, AND CUSPIDORS, in Class 33, Glassware, and presents herewith five (5) facsimiles showing the trade-mark as actually used by applicant upon the goods, and requests that the same be registered in the United States Patent Office in accordance with the act of February 20, 1905, as amended. The trade-mark has been continuously used and applied to said goods in applicant's business since June 11, 1938. The trade-mark is applied to the goods by forming the mark in the glassware by a pressing operation.

Prior registration No. 329,022, issued October 15, 1935, is now owned by applicant.

The undersigned hereby appoints Corbett & Mahoney, register No. 13,144, (a firm composed of Edwin P. Corbett and John J. Mahoney) whose postal address is 820-822 Huntington Bank Building, Columbus, Ohio, its attorneys, to prosecute this application for registration, with full powers of substitution and revocation, to make alterations and amendments therein, to sign its name to the drawing, to receive the certificate, and to transact all business in the Patent Office connected therewith.

ANCHOR HOCKING GLASS
CORPORATION.
By WILLIAM V. FISHER,
Vice-President.

Patent application for the "anchor over H" emblem.

Registered Feb. 12, 1946   **Trade-Mark 419,329**

UNITED STATES PATENT OFFICE

Anchor Hocking Glass Corporation, Lancaster, Ohio

Act of February 20, 1905

Application May 5, 1945, Serial No. 483,015

Anchorglass

STATEMENT

To the Commissioner of Patents:

Anchor Hocking Glass Corporation, a corporation duly organized under the laws of the State of Delaware, located at Lancaster, Ohio, and doing business at Lancaster, Ohio, has adopted and used the trade-mark shown in the accompanying drawing, for GLASS ARTICLES—NAMELY, JARS, BOTTLES, JUGS, GLASSES, CUPS, SAUCERS, PLATES, TRAYS, DISHES, AND COOKING UTENSILS—in Class 33, Glassware, and presents herewith five (5) facsimiles showing the trade-mark as actually used by applicant upon the goods and requests that the same be registered in the United States Patent Office in accordance with the act of February 20, 1905. The trade-mark has been continuously used and applied to said goods in applicant's business since March 15, 1945. The trade-mark is applied or affixed to the goods or to the packages containing the same by molding the mark in the glassware or by printing or stenciling the mark on the packages containing the same.

Applicant is the owner of trade-mark registration No. 329,022 issued to Salem Glass Works on October 15, 1935, and of trade-mark registration No. 376,781, issued to applicant on April 9, 1940.

The undersigned hereby appoints Norman N. Holland (registry No. 11,940), whose post-office address is Two Rector Street, New York 6, New York, its attorney, to prosecute this application for registration with full power of substitution and revocation, and to make alterations and amendments therein, to receive the certificate, and to transact all business in the Patent Office connected therewith.

ANCHOR HOCKING GLASS
CORPORATION.
By WILLIAM V. FISHER,
President.

Patent application for the words "Anchorglass."

Identification Marks

Over the years, Anchor Hocking has used several identification marks on their glassware. In 1980, the company issued a limited edition 75th anniversary ashtray, pictured below, which portrays the corporate identification marks. During the photographing, the marks on the ashtray were blackened with a magic marker so they would show up when photographed. Originally, when the Hocking Glass Company was established in 1905, the company used the mark seen on the left side of the ashtray. This mark was used from 1905 until 1937, when it was replaced by the more familiar anchor over H mark (center of ashtray) to illustrate the merger of the Hocking Glass Company and the Anchor Cap Company. Finally, in October 1977, the company adopted a new symbol (right side of the ashtray), an anchor with a modern, contemporary appearance to further the new corporate identity.

Not all Royal Ruby glassware was identified by marks incorporated directly into the glass. At least three styles of paper labels were attached to glassware items. Two of the label designs were made in both a gold and silver version.

75th Anniversary ashtray.

Crystal ashtray, 5 1/2" in diameter, $50-55 with original box.

Paper label with "Royal Ruby" only.

126

Paper label which states "Royal Ruby Anchorglass, Anchor Hocking Glass Corp., Lancaster Ohio, U.S.A."

Paper label which states "Royal Ruby Anchorglass, Anchor Hocking Glass Corp., Lancaster Ohio, U.S.A." Notice this label was made in the gold version.

Paper label which states "Royal Ruby Anchorglass, Anchor Hocking Glass Corp., Lancaster Ohio, U.S.A." Notice this label was made in the silver version.

Paper label for the Gay Fad Studios located in Lancaster, Ohio. The label states "Gay Fad hand decorated, fired for permanency." This is the only Gay Fad label I have seen and it was attached to a Hazel Atlas pitcher.

Request for Additional Information

I am always seeking information concerning Anchor Hocking's Royal Ruby glassware. Much of the information about Royal Ruby is not available outside the company. This book will undoubtedly be updated, and it is imperative new information be made available to collectors. Feel free to contact me at the following address:

Philip L. Hopper
1120 Choctaw Ridge Road
Midwest City, OK 73130-6129
Phone: (405) 732-6624
E-mail: rrglass@swbell.net

Please be patient if you need a response. I am not in the glassware business. I am a military officer first and a collector the rest of the time. I will make every effort to provide prompt feedback on your inquiries.

Index